KU-706-111

Contents Copyright © 2005

Published by RUG HOOKING MAGAZINE, 5067 Ritter Road, Mechanicsburg, PA 17055
www.rughookingmagazine.com

Printed in U.S.A.

10 9 8 7 6 5 4 3

First edition

INTRODUCTION

On February 27, 1998, I attended my first rug hooking workshop. I arrived as the person in charge unlocked the building. The two of us only chatted a few minutes before our attention was riveted to a "tornadic" whirl of red hair sweeping through the door. It was the workshop teacher, Jane Olson. Being the only one under 70, I helped unload the van … and have been doing so ever since.

Jane Selen started hooking in the mid 1930s. Her mother, a regular student of Pearl K. McGown, only liked to hook the designs in the rugs she made. Therefore, Jane was recruited to hook all the backgrounds, when she wasn't working in her father's bakery in Worcester, Massachusetts. "Since all I got to do was the boring part, I pretty much hated hooking", says Jane. Still, she hooked regularly until she left home to get married to a World War II flyer, Bert Olson. When they moved to California in 1957, the accidental discovery of a traditional rug hooking

much more than information about the pattern in question. Almost every issue also has general hooking instructions, dye recipes and suggestions, Q & A's, letters from readers, critiques and rug hooking news from around the country. She has even made it a practice to regularly include lists of *other* teachers you can and should consult. While the *Rugger's Roundtable* certainly has promoted Jane's business, its main agenda has always been to promote traditional rug hooking in general. Jane never keeps a secret very long—once learned it goes into the *Rugger's Roundtable* so everyone can take advantage of the tip. It's no wonder that one of the biggest subscriber sections for the newsletter has always been other rug hooking teachers. In fact, many of these teachers buy complete reprints of all Jane's *Rugger's Roundtables* so they can use them as instructional manuals for their students. Over the years, it is those teachers who have begun to call Jane's work *The Rug Hooker's Bible*, consulting it faithfully

"While this may be the way that I suggest you hook something, don't be afraid to experiment because you may find a way that works better for you."

class in the immediate neighborhood stirred artistic juices deep within and Jane once again, picked up a hook. This time, she got to do the whole rug. Shortly thereafter, the teacher retired and Jane was asked to take over the class. Before much longer she was teaching a wide variety of fiber arts, including rug hooking, for the LA County Adult Education System, as well as offering hooking classes out of her home. Her business was expanded with the purchase of Mildred Sprout's rug patterns in 1972 and Clarisse McLain's swatch line in 1976. It was also in 1976 that she restarted the *Rugger's Roundtable*, a bimonthly newsletter originally begun by Mildred Sprout to promote patterns that she offered for sale.

Jane Olson's *Rugger's Roundtable* continued to promote a new pattern with each issue. However, Jane's approach has always been to provide

when needing inspiration and help.

Given the fact that the newsletter has grown and evolved over a 30-year period, it is not surprising to learn that information on most topics can be scattered over the complete 30 year run. After all, she did not set out to write a progressive work on rug hooking. Looking through all the copies of the *Rugger's Roundtable* will necessitate that you flip through at least three large loose-leaf notebooks of issues, consulting a few different indexes as you go. The upside of a search like this provides one with a wealth of information on traditional rug hooking and the progression of our art form over the last three decades. The downside of such a search is that it is almost too much information to easily navigate. Many topics are repeated, some of her opinions change over time (others never will), and quite a

The Rug Hooker's Bible

The best from 30 years of Jane Olson's Rugger's Roundtable

Gene's Scroll, 16" x 11", #8-cut wool on monk's cloth.
Designed by Jane Olson and Gene Shepherd.
Hooked by Gene Shepherd, Anaheim, California, 2005.

Edited and expanded by Gene Shepherd

Photography by Gene Shepherd

TABLE OF CONTENTS

bit of the current events reported—while historically interesting to fiber artists—take up a lot of space. The goal of this edit is to organize and repackage the essence of Jane's experience with out destroying its "heart." That's where I come into the picture.

These days I am allowed to do more than load and unload the van. I now team teach with her once a month in Anaheim, California, and she teaches for me each year at Cambria Pines Rug Camp. In addition, we seem to continually collaborate on a multiplicity of fiber art projects—hooking, dyeing, and designing as well as providing rug hooking instruction to children and multiethnic groups here and abroad. As stated, Jane has made a habit of promoting new teachers over the years, and I am an excellent example of that generous attitude. We get along very well together because our philosophical approach to rug hooking is pretty much the same. Then again, if you can't trust your pastor to edit and expand *The Rug Hooker's Bible*, whom can you trust? However, we do differ in certain areas. Jane has spent most of her time hooking with cuts #3-6, with those of #3 and #4 being, by far, her most usual preference. My preference is #6 through #10. She uses lots of 6-value swatches, I use almost none, preferring left over scraps to new wool. She holds her hook one way, and I hold it another. Still, a careful read through *The Rugger's Roundtable* proves that Jane's triple-decade mantra has always been: "While this may be the way that I suggest you hook something, don't be afraid to experiment because you may find a way that works better for you." A strict interpretation of that message would say that my dissimilar style, a way that works better for me, is precisely in line with what she has been preaching all along. Although much care has been given to provide you with the best instruction and information that we can, we have also worked very hard to give you a multiplicity of suggestions that will encourage you to *"find the way that works best for you."*

This work is not intended to be historically

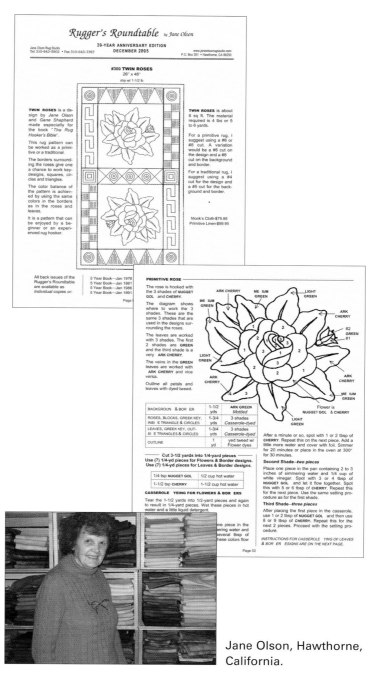

Jane Olson, Hawthorne, California.

limited to the issues of *The Rugger's Roundtable* that have appeared in print. I often provide information that has not been previously addressed as well as make liberal contributions throughout, and Jane has also added new material. In all things, including the new issue exclusive to this publication, we have collaborated to provide the reader with as many options as possible. It's been a joy to do this as we both love rug hooking, the opportunity of sharing our art form, and each other.—*Gene Shepherd*

FROM THE EDITOR

For over 30 years, Jane Olson has taught rug hooking to rug hookers of all levels—beginners as well as advanced. Throughout her decades of experience, she has produced a quarterly newsletter known as the *Rugger's Roundtable.* This indispensable newsletter became the "Bible" for many students, who would refer (and still do) to each issue for dyeing tips, hooking techniques, care and cleaning advice, what to do with leftover selvages, and more.

Now Jane Olson and Gene Shepherd have collaborated on *The Rug Hooker's Bible,* an updated and expanded book containing the best information from Jane's newsletter, plus the very latest techniques for hooking a rug from beginning to end. See how the same designs can be hooked in four different ways—fine shaded, primitive outline and fill, dip-dyed, and leftover scraps. *The Rug Hooker's Bible* includes answers to questions about what kind of equipment to use, backings to pick, dye recipes and shortcuts, how to hook circles, squares, triangles, backgrounds, and so much more. This exciting, easy-to-use reference guide contains information for all rug hookers. You won't want to be without it.

Jane's hooking and design abilities are legendary in the rug hooking community. Learn from the master as you read this book and discover how uncomplicated hooking can be, if you just follow her tips. For those who have questions and would like clear, concise answers, this beautifully illustrated book written in an easy-to-read format, will open the door to an exciting future in the art of rug hooking. Enjoy reading *Rug Hooking* magazine's newest addition to the rug hooking library. Remember, the sky is the limit!—*Ginny Stimmel*

ABOUT THE AUTHOR

Gene Shepherd is director of Cambria Pines Rug Camp, always held the first full week of June at Cambria Pines Lodge, Cambria, California. He particularly enjoys designing rugs and doing commission work for individuals and historic museums. Gene regularly teaches private and group classes in Anaheim, California and has also taught at the ATHA Biennial. Known for his particular passion of introducing rug hooking to multi-ethnic children and adults, he has traveled as far as Moscow, Russia, to teach this art form. He is a frequent contributor to *Rug Hooking* magazine where his hooked rugs have been featured several times there and in the ATHA magazine. Three of his original works have been chosen to appear in *A Celebration of Hand Hooked Rugs*: **Fog** in 2002, **Russian Birch** in 2004, and **Miss Weigle** in 2005. **Russian Birch** was also chosen as a Reader's Choice finalist. In 2003, he served as one of four judges for *A Celebration of Hand-Hooked Rugs XIII*. Although most of Gene's work is based on his original designs, he recently re-created two rugs for the U.S. Park Service. Working with black and white archival photos he designed and hooked two rugs that had been lost from Franklin Delano

Gene Shepherd, Anaheim, California.

Roosevelt's Top Cottage at Hyde Park, New York. These rugs went on display at Hyde Park in 2004. Gene resides in Anaheim, California with his wife, Marsha, and daughter, Ann. He is senior pastor at Anaheim First Christian Church.

For a gallery of Gene's work, teaching schedule, original patterns, links to companion sites, or information about Cambria Pines Rug Camp, log on to his website at www.geneshepherd.com.

Gene Shepherd, Fiber Artist
108 N. Vine
Anaheim, CA 92805
714.956.5150
gene@geneshepherd.com

The Tools We Need To Hook

Exotica, 33" x 43", #3, 4, and 5-cut wool on monk's cloth. Designed and hooked by Jane Olson, Hawthorne, California, 2000.

A Good Foundation

A hooked rug is made by pulling loops of material through some sort of foundation fabric. That fabric must be strong enough to withstand the pressure created by thousands of loops which will invade it, as well as the feet that will walk on it decade after decade. For this reason, the choice of a proper fabric backing is very important. Your rug will only be as strong as its backing. These are the most common options and what we have discovered when using them:

A burlap foundation guarantees that your piece will eventually fall apart...you'll never be sorry if you **avoid** burlap.

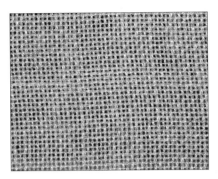

■ **Burlap**—Burlap (called Hessian in England) is made of twisted jute or sisal fibers. It was an early and natural choice for hooked rug backing because of its availability and the ease with which fabric strips can be pulled through it in loops. In the early 19th century many a burlap sack was opened and recycled into a rug pattern. Lots of rug artists still like to use it today, although neither Jane or I are among the ranks of supporters. Both jute and sisal are processed in such a way that some natural chemicals from the plant cling to the fibers. While this initially helps the fibers bond to each other, the dual effect of light and age change these chemicals to an acid, which eventually destroys the burlap. A burlap foundation guarantees that your piece will eventually fall apart. As Mary Klotz says, "Burlap is really good for landscapers who want to wrap tree roots before they plant them, however, it is terrible for rugs!" To be fair, modern burlap is certainly superior to the old stuff used by our grandparents; however, it still breaks in much the same ways as its ancestors. Jane has always offered patterns on burlap because some customers insist on using it, although according to her, this is not the place to skimp. "Why would you want to go

through all that work on a piece of burlap that will just fall apart too soon?" She also goes so far as to say that if a burlap pattern has been folded for more than six months it weakens at the folds and should be thrown away. Burlap rugs usually do break apart first on the edge, where the burlap is folded. We know of rugs on burlap that have torn right down the middle from nothing more than normal use. You'll never be sorry if you avoid burlap.

While it is related to the burlap fibers mentioned above, it [linen] is processed in such a way that no harmful chemicals remain on the fibers.

■ **Linen**—Linen backing, made from twisted flax fibers, has also been around for along time. It has some of the look and feel of burlap, as well as being wide loop friendly. Linen fiber is also strong, particularly when wet. While it is related to the burlap fibers mentioned above, it is processed in such a way that no harmful chemicals remain on the fibers. Linen is available in a variety of weaves in bleached and natural colors. For artists that like to do cuts #8 and above, a primitive or looser weave of linen has a real appeal, particularly for #9 and #10-cut. I find myself using it more and more as it is the easiest backing to work with for those two cuts. However, people who use gripper type frames will find that linen often doesn't want to stick to their frames as well as other backings. Since linen usually comes off the bolt a little stiffer than cotton backings, it may need to be stretched "square," before taking off a pattern. Those who draw their own patterns will find that it is much more difficult to draw on linen. While the natural colors of linen tend to soak up more ink making the lines harder to see, the bleached varieties do allow the pattern line to be more pronounced. For those who use a light box when tracing patterns, it's more difficult to see the pattern lines shining through the tighter weave linens than the looser or primitive ones. Finally, linen is also more expensive, usually half as much as other backings. Still, its supporters are legion, however, Jane isn't one of them.

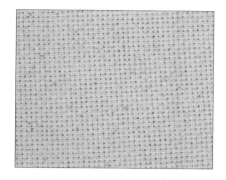

■ **Rug Warp**—Rug warp is made from hard twisted cotton threads. It is much heavier in feel than other cotton backings. Under normal use, it's hard to imagine a rug that is made on this backing could ever wear out. However, because it is constructed of tightly woven larger threads, it is not a hospitable backing for wider cuts. There just isn't enough room for them. In fact, it only seems to work appropriately when used for #3 and #4-cut. It would be a great choice for about anything using these cuts.

The complaint most often heard about monk's cloth is that it stretches.

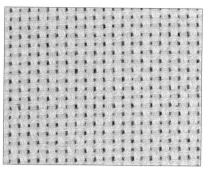

■ **Monk's Cloth**—Monk's cloth is also made from cotton. In appearance it has the same weave structure as aida cloth for counted cross stitch, only made of bigger threads. This backing will work for every size cut, although a #10 pushes its limit. It costs more than burlap, but less than linen. Always consistently woven, it even has a periodic white thread, which comes in very handy when doing geometrics. It also clings well to gripper frames. Monk's cloth is easy to mark on and shows its lines very well. The complaint most often heard about monk's cloth is that it stretches. This comment always puzzles us as we both have more trouble with other backings wanting to stretch. Of course, all the fabrics listed will stretch if you pull them hard enough, but both of us use monk's cloth for nearly everything we do and neither of us has trouble with it stretching.

Synthetic homespun is quite good for projects where you only want to hook a shape with no hooked backgrounds.

■ **Synthetic Homespun**—Synthetic homespun looks, feels, and acts almost like burlap, without the irregularity that burlap usually provides. It's quite good for projects where you only want to hook a shape with no hooked background. However, it doesn't seem to stick to gripper type frames as well as the cotton backings. You also need to be careful when blocking a finished piece. If the iron is too hot, the synthetic fibers will melt.

Truth be told, you can hook through almost any fabric. Some artists, who do their own sewing, make wool jackets and then hook designs through the yoke or pocket. Others have hooked designs through crocheted and knitted sweaters. While all of these things would work fine for the article mentioned, floor rugs should be hooked on one of the above mentioned rug backings. ●

BE PICKY WHEN PICKING A PATTERN

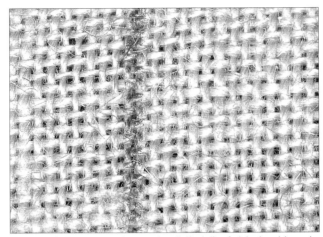

The dark line runs down the "ditch" of this backing. It never jumps out of the line of holes in which it starts.

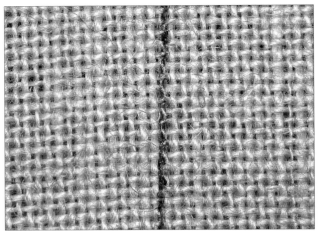

The dark line in this photo jumps from the ditch where it starts in at the top, to the next ditch over by the time it gets to the bottom of the picture. That may not seem like much difference. However, given the scale of this photo, that change takes place in a little over one inch. If the pattern's border edge line changes even a ditch or two every few inches, it will cause big problems.

Most people buy their patterns already on a backing. If you have a backing preference, be sure to communicate that with the designer when ordering. Most designers and suppliers are willing to work with you to get a backing that you like.

When buying a pattern, make sure that it is printed "square" on the backing. That means that each of the four sides of the pattern should run exactly in or next to a straight "ditch" of holes. This is an area where there should be no compromise.

When borderlines do not run in the ditch, the whole pattern will be out of kilter. This is particularly critical for geometrics since all of those internal lines also must jive up with each other. If you have the opportunity to inspect a pattern before buying, take a careful look. Before

ordering a pattern, particularly from someone you have never used before, ask about the return policy. You will want to return a pattern that is not printed square.

To make your own pattern, use a permanent marker to draw the design on a good piece of thin white paper. Pin the backing over the top side of the pattern in several places so it can not slip. (If the design has straight sides, draw them first on the backing, making sure each row stays in its appropriate ditch. Then pin over design.) Place the pattern/backing on a light box and redraw the lines on the backing with a permanent marker. A glass top table tape with a lamp under it or a sliding glass door on a sunny day will both work in a pinch.

Secure the edge of a pattern so it

will not fray. Go around all four sides with either a zigzag stitch, masking tape folded over the edge, or a bead of white glue. The edge of a credit card can be used to force the glue into the weave of the backing, squeegee fashion. Let the glue dry before hooking. ●

DEALING WITH WOOL

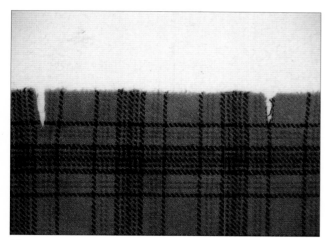

These nicks are placed parallel to the selvage on the original edge of the fabric. The person who dyed the wool placed them there so you can tear or cut with your cutter in the same direction as the selvage. If you prepare your own wool, it's a good idea to make these little notches as it sometimes gets confusing where the selvage was.

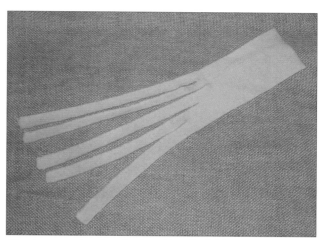

Ripping wool strips for hooking is fairly easy to do if the wool is good. It really only works well for a #10 cut (¹/₂") or wider. Just notch your wool across the top at half-inch intervals and then tear it into strips. If the wool will not tear, you are using the wrong wool.

■ **Tearing**—Wool must be torn into manageable pieces that will easily go through a cutter. When working with large pieces off the bolt, notch where you want to cut, then tear by hand. Repeat this process for half and quarter yard pieces. Tearing wool is better than cutting as it will tear "straight" with the weave of the wool. Cutting with scissors or rotary cutters, like one would with normal fabric, causes the cut to go across threads instead of with the thread.

■ **Buying**—When buying smaller pieces of wool—less than a yard— they will most often come with little notches or nicks along one side.

Why should anyone care where the selvage was? When using narrow cuts, it's a good idea to always cut the wool strips in the same direction as the selvage—that would be the length of the entire bolt, not the

width. The weave on narrow wool strips usually hangs together better when cut this way. Also, some tweeds or twills tend to be much stronger when cut in a direction parallel with the selvage or warp threads. The decorative skips in the weft threads

(the width of the bolt) often do not support the weave structure like the warp threads (the length of the bolt) do. It's probably a good idea to just get used to cutting that way. However, for wider cuts, particularly #7 and up, it really doesn't make any difference what direction the wool goes through your cutter.

■ **Equipment**—You do not have to

have expensive equipment to make hooked rugs. Many people have spent their entire rug hooking life hand ripping or cutting their wool strips with a pair of scissors. People often ask if they can't just use a rotary cutter. The answer is, of course you can.

You do not have to have expensive equipment to make hooked rugs.

However, both scissor and rotary cuts are very difficult to repeat with the exactness one would like for rug hooking, particularly with the narrower cuts. Then, there is the actual pain such scissor repetition causes to one's hands. You can do it, but most people find it unacceptable over the long run. ●

While they come in a variety of styles and prices, cutters tend to either sit or clamp on a table. Recommending a cutter is very difficult because, like so much else in life, you get what you pay for.

Moderately priced models tend to use a head of blades or sharp ridges.

More expensive ones use pressure bands like a crank operated pasta machine.

A nut must be removed from this cutter every time the head is changed. To do so, place the wrench on the nut and rotate the handle counterclockwise until the nut comes off. The wrench will stop when it hits the floor of the cutter, providing enough pressure to loosen the nut.

On the 8th day, God created cutters. Also called cloth slitters or strippers, these little mechanical marvels make repetitive cutting relatively easy. Cutter heads are based on a $1/32$" scale. Therefore, a #3-cut is $3/32$" wide. This is true up to #8, which is $8/32$" or $1/4$" wide. Cut #9 is half again as wide as #8, so it is $12/32$" wide and #10 is twice as big as #8, or $16/32$" ($1/2$") wide. Most people think it is just easier to have cutter heads to sort all that out.

Almost every cutter has its pros and cons. Since cutter design will probably determine your attitude towards your cutter, it's best to contemplate their differences before buying.

■ **Cost**—Cost is the first big divide when shopping for cutters. No cutter, unless found used in a thrift store, is cheap. Still, this one-time investment will probably bring more hooking happiness than any single purchase. They fall into two categories—moderate, less than $200, and expensive $400 and up. If cost is not an issue, go with the more expensive brands as they are easier and quicker to use. However, regardless of price, the cheaper ones cut wool strips equally as well as the expensive ones.

Cutter mechanisms vary from cutter to cutter. Again, each works fine,. however, the head with ridges tends to stick to the wool the longer it is used, necessitating frequent cleaning. That can be done by running a fabric softener sheet through the cutter. The pressure bands, on the other hand, never seem to be affected by that buildup. It is annoying to always stop and clean the heads, but it must be done.

■ **Changing Cut Size**—Changing cut size is accomplished in a variety of ways. Again, you pay for ease. Cutters in the moderate price range tend to have cutting heads that are secured by a metal nut.

■ **Tightening**—To tighten, put the nut on with your fingers and then place the wrench on it. Turn the handle clockwise. The wrench will once again hit the floor of the cutter. Continue to turn until the handle does not want to turn. Then, tighten for no more than a quarter turn, just enough to snug it up. Many a cutter has been ruined because someone overtightened the nut.

The more expensive cutters either have heads that easily slip in and out, or contain multiple heads that simply rotate to the size you want.

■ **Tension**—Tension is vital to cutting operations, as the wool will not cut completely through without it. Moderate priced cutters have a knob somewhere that allows you to adjust the tension.

■ **Attaching**—Cutters attach to your workspace by either sitting on it or clamping to it. Cutters that just sit on the table tend to move around while cutting, until one gets the hang of holding them down with a thumb.

Clamp on cutters do not shift around when cutting. However, with the new lightweight plastic tables, it's becoming harder and harder at hook-ins to find a table that is thin enough to accept the clamp of the cutter.

■ **Wool Guides**—Wool guides are necessary if one is to achieve perfect cuts. Most cutters have a built in edge, next to which you push the wool when being cut. The actual

On this model, the different heads just slip in and out. They pop into place and can only fit the "right" way.

Cut size is embossed on only one side of the cutter head. That side must face out so it can be seen when the head is placed back on the cutter bolt.

On this model, the tension nob is on the underneath side. You must loosen the tension before installing a head and then readjust afterwards. Sometimes, depending on the thickness of the wool being cut, tension must be increased in order to make a complete cut. When the wool is perforated, instead of cut, the tension knob needs to be tightened. The more expensive models are factory set to the proper tension and never need to be adjusted.

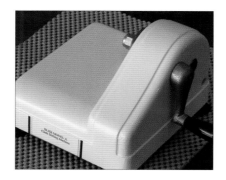

Placing the cutter on a little non-skid rubber mat will help provide stability, however, it doesn't take the place of just learning how to hold it. This cutter will go almost anywhere and it will sit still, once you get the feel of it.

People often carry a wooden base for their clamp on cutters. This guarantees the perfect base any time and any place they want to cut wool.

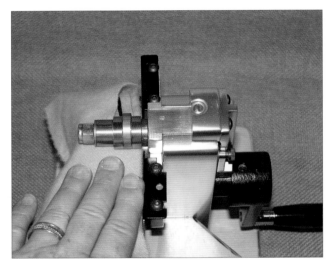

As you crank the wool through, try to keep the edge of the wool touching the inner guide. If it rides up on the guide, the inside piece will be a little fat. If it doesn't touch the guide, the inside piece will be a bit narrow.

cutter heads are spaced according to that edge. A few models have a guide, which you must set every time you change cut sizes. This is very annoying and time consuming. Another model requires you to set the guide just once in the cutter's life, which is more palatable.

■ **Multiple Heads**—Multiple heads at the same time are standard on some cutters. That means that more than one cutting option is set up and available at any given time. On the more expensive cutters, as many as three heads are permanently mounted and rotated as needed. While they can never be changed, they are easy

to access. If you want more cutter options, another cutter must be bought. Some cheaper cutters allow for two heads to be installed at one time. They can be taken off and replaced by loosening the nuts, etc. Again, the guides have to be set each time.

■ **Cutting**—Cutting wool with all cutters is a fairly simple affair once they are set up and ready to operate. Wool pieces ought to be no wider than about 6" by any length you want. Wider pieces than 6" tend to want to hang off the side of the cutter while you are trying to get it to evenly proceed through the cutter.

After the wool goes through the first time, take the end that went through last and rotate it so it will go through first the next pass. Keep rotating so that the end going through the cutter last becomes the end going through the cutter first the next time. This rotation helps keep your wool squared up . . . or, at least we think it does. ●

For maximum effectiveness, patterns must be stretched on some sort of frame. Your set up can be something as simple as a pattern thumb tacked to the backside of a garage sale picture frame. I used my wife's quilt frames for my first project. Frames tend to come in three basic varieties: hoop, scroll, and gripper.

■ Hoop Style Frames—Hoop style frames are made out of wooden hoops. To use, the hoops are moved around on the pattern to the desired section. When it comes time to reposition the hoop, most people find the job to be more difficult than with other styles of frames. If the bolt at the back of the hoop is too short, it will be difficult to open the hoop wide enough to slip over a partially hooked rug. Of course, the bolt can be replaced with one that is longer. While some very experienced rug hookers use only a hoop, it seems to work best for people who want to try rug hooking without investing a lot of money. They normally choose something else for their second project. If you use this sort of frame, it seems to work best for smaller cuts.

■ Scroll Frames—Scroll frames have two moveable bars that allow the pattern to be rolled up. Initially, the pattern must be secured to the bar with thumbtacks.

■ Gripper Type Frames—Gripper type frames make use of carding strips on all four top sides of the frame. These frames are great for small projects. They also work very well for room size rugs as the frame can just be moved under the rug from spot to spot. Gripper frames can

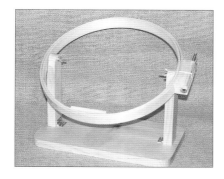

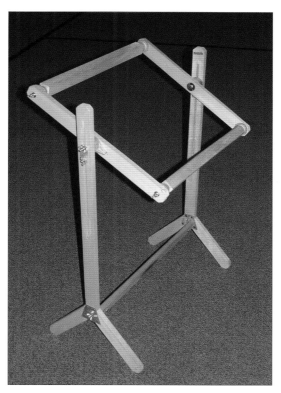

Hoops used for rug hooking need to be wider and stronger than normal embroidery hoops. While some rug hookers get by with just a hoop, most prefer to have the hoop mounted on some sort of base. If using a hoop, make sure it is between 12" and 18" wide, with 14" or 16" being optimum. This sort of frame is fairly economical and easy to stick in a suitcase.

This type of frame is wider than other options, allowing the artist a bigger space in which to work. Scroll frames are perfect when the pattern is a close fit. When the pattern is either much larger or much smaller, it makes use of this sort of frame difficult. It's also a challenge to tack the pattern in "square" to the frame. For decades, Jane used this type of frame. However, she never rolled her patterns. Instead, she would thumb tack a section of her oversized pattern on the top of all four sides. When that part was hooked, she would reposition.

be held on one's lap, set on a table or mounted to a floor stand. Their smaller size allows you to rotate the frame while hooking. While they are superior to all other types, they also cost more money. They are made by professional rug supply companies as well as hobbyists. Given the puncturing quality of these frames, it is best to cover them with something, like a terry hand towel, when traveling or not in use. Many rug hookers are

adding carding strips to old floor frames. This allows easy pattern instillation as well as an increased work area. Do not try to attach the strips with anything less than a high-powered compressed air staple gun.

Gripper frames need occasional cleaning. The teeth collect bits of wool and lint.

Most frames types can be purchased (or adapted) so that they either stand-alone or sit in your lap. ●

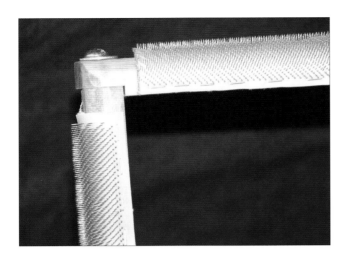

The little teeth grip the backing and hold the pattern in place. Some frames require you to slightly stretch the fabric as you lay it on the frame. On others, the pattern is positioned and then stretched by a vertical and horizontal arm.

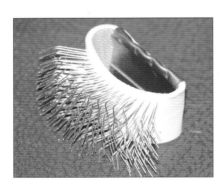

A thin wire brush will sweep through the natural rows of the metal teeth and remove the bits of fluff. Keeping the carding strips free of lint allows them to hold the pattern better. It's best to do this simple process outside.

Lap frames sit in your lap or on a table. They can be used in the car or easily carried from place to place.

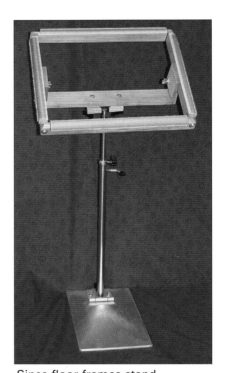

Since floor frames stand independent of the artist, both hands are completely free for hooking. Many of them adjust, swivel, turn, bob and make grilled cheese sandwiches. This particular model easily breaks down to fit in a carry on bag. This is our frame of choice.

WHAT YOU NEED TO KNOW ABOUT HOOKS

Hooks come in all shapes and sizes. Each style has its devotees. Experiment to find which one works best for you. After all, no two hands are exactly alike. When picking out a hook, do not make your choice based on how it looks. Close your eyes and choose the hook based on how it feels in your hand. If possible, ask the supplier to let you take it for a test run and hook a few loops. The more the hook handle fills your hand, the less cramping or fatigued your hand will feel. If the handle is too small for your hand, you'll have to work harder at gripping it, causing more tension.

Hooks are usually held in one of two ways: pencil style or palmed.

■ **Pencil Style**—The pencil style makes your hand do all the work, while giving it less to grip. While it can work well for narrow cuts, it is not a good idea for the wide ones.

■ **Palming Style**—By palming a hook, one can take advantage of the lever action the hook handle is supposed to provide. Think of it as prying loops through the backing as opposed to pulling them.

Regardless of how others hold hooks, the right way is the way that works for you. When you find a comfortable way to hold your hook, don't let anyone badger you into changing it.

Hook Options Abound

■ **Crochet Hooks**—Crochet hooks can be used for rug hooking. However, there just isn't enough of a handle to grip without causing a lot of tension and fatigue in your hand and forearm. Used as is, it will cause you a lot of physical pain. Yarn stores

The pencil style of holding a hook.

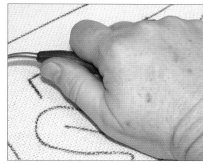

The palming style of holding a hook.

Pencil type hooks are crochet hooks with long skinny handles.

often sell a sponge like sleeve that will make the handle bigger and easier to grip. If you have small hands, this extra material may be enough to work for you. People with big hands will probably need to steer away from this type of hook.

■ **Pencil Type Hooks**—Pencil type hooks are crochet hooks with long, skinny handles. They are normally held as one would hold a pencil. Held in this way, they are fine for smaller

cuts. Pencil hooks can be palmed for wider cuts; however, skinny handles are much more difficult to grip than fatter ones, thereby increasing hand tension.

■ **Wood Handle Hooks**—Hooks with traditional wood handles have been around for a long time.

It's good they come in all sizes and shapes because hookers come that way too. Again, go with what feels good to you, not what looks pretty.

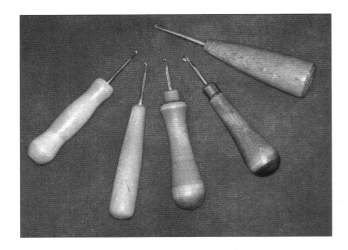

Hooks with traditional wood handles.

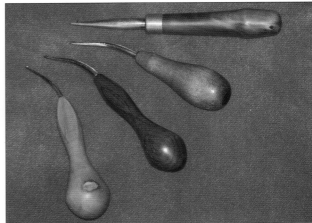

Cutting and hooking creates a lot of dust and lint. A nylon net pot scrubber doubles as an effective rug brush. Use it often to keep the dust off the surface of your hooking.

I regularly hook with #3-#10 cuts and use four different sized hooks. I use my smaller hook for cuts #3-#5, a bigger hook for #6 and #7, one just reserved for #8 and a jumbo hook for #9 and #10.

Bent-handled scissors

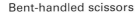

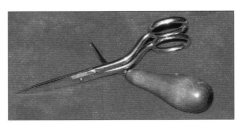

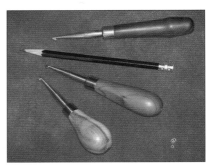

Jumbo loops need to be pulled with jumbo hooks.

Size matters, almost as much as picking the handle style that works for you. Generally speaking, smaller hooks are used for smaller cuts. Medium hooks are used for medium cuts, etc. Jane has used just one hook for decades and does not think it is necessary to have several hooks. However, most of her hooking is confined to #3-#6 cuts.

■ **Jumbo Loops**—Jumbo loops need to be pulled with a jumbo hook. When hooking cuts #9 and #10 do not settle for a hook with a shaft size smaller than eight or nine millimeters. It ought to look approximately as thick as a pencil. A thicker shaft opens up a bigger hole, thereby making it easier to pull up a wide loop. Sure, it can be done with something smaller, however, your wrist and

forearm will pay for it. Hooks are supposed to make our work easier. A jumbo hook, pushed in all the way to the wooden handle, will greatly reduce the effort it takes to pull those big loops. Jumbo hooks can also come in handy should you ever need to defend yourself at a rowdy guild meeting.

■ **Hook Shafts**—Hook shafts come straight or bent. The theory behind the bent shaft is that less effort needs to be expended to push it through the hole when held in the palm, since it is closer to the hole than a straight shaft. To do this, move your whole arm in shuttle like fashion, instead of working your wrist. There is also the added benefit of using your palm to push the hook through the backing. I find I have less

trouble with my wrist and forearm when using this type of hook and strongly urge new hookers learn how.

■ **Scissors**—Good scissors are a must for rug hooking. Since most of the cutting we do needs to leave a squared-off tail in line with the loops of the rug, bent handled scissors provide the best option. Their design allows the artist to simply sit the scissors flat on the rug and snip. Regular scissors cannot get that low and usually come in at an angle.

There is no discussion on this topic. Buy the best pair of bent handled scissors you can afford and keep them sharp. ●

Antique Geometric with Flowers, 32" x 60", #6-cut wool on monk's cloth. Adapted from antique pattern and hooked by Gene Shepherd, Anaheim, California, 2001.

Wool provides the best fabric for hooking if you are making a rug that is going to go on the floor. It's true that antique rugs contain all sorts of recycled fabric—they used whatever they had, particularly if it was a color they needed. However, we are looking for what is best, since recycling is not necessarily our foremost concern. Wool is strong and dirt resistant, compared to other fabric. When going for longevity, wool will always be your best choice. Hooking the entire rug with wool greatly increases the chance that it will wear

Plaids and checks are the wools you can't live with or without.

and fade evenly over the years.

Since each fabric wears differently, mixing fabrics in floor rugs increases the chance that the rug will not wear in an even fashion. Should you want to use some other medium for a floor rug, for example knit T-shirts, do the entire rug with that fabric.

Picking appropriate wool is important because not all wool is equally good for hooking. Hooking wool is normally described as "flannel weight" wool. It weighs $3/4$ of a pound per yard. Since most wool is not marked that way, it's important to learn what "feels" right. It does not take too long before an experienced hooker can tell if the piece is the right weight. It's heavier than suit wool and thinner than blanket wool. Another test to use on wool is to see if it will easily tear. If it tears without too much trouble and without falling apart at the edge, it will probably be fine to hook.

■ **Plaids**—Since plaids provide such great variety when hooked, fiber artists are always searching for interesting textured wool. However, the very weave structures that create this interest often produce wool fabric that simply wants to fall apart

when cut into strips.

Wool that will not easily tear without leaving a decidedly ragged edge is wool that will be hard to hook. This problem is compounded the narrower one goes with cut size and lessens the higher one goes with cut size. Wool selection often comes down to how much of that particular wool is needed. If an entire background is to be hooked, save yourself a lot of time and trouble and pick wool that rips without causing a mess. If you just need a little bit of that special something, then even bad hooking wool can be tolerated for effect. Sometimes loosely woven tweed can be run through the washing machine and dryer to good effect. Two minutes of agitation followed by a hot dryer often makes fabric shrink just enough to be useable. Fortunately, even bad wool can generally be used as a #10 cut.

■ **Wall Hangings**—Hooked pieces not intended for the floor are another matter. Since they won't be abused by foot traffic, anything that suits your fancy is acceptable. Silk saris, ribbons, gold lame, wool roving, leatherette, and nubby yarns are just a few of the many possibilities for

achieving an interesting effect. Remember, when selecting a hanging place, different fibers will not fade the same way. It's best not to hang a hooked piece in direct sunlight anyway. Also, while we normally want the loops in floor rugs to be the same size, once a piece is dedicated to an off the floor use, interesting effects can be created with loops of different sizes.

■ **Good Lighting**—A well-lighted work area will make hooking easier. If you have the option, choose a spot for daytime hooking that is bathed in soft natural light. If you must rely on artificial light, choose something that does not affect color.

■ **A Good Chair**—Relieve stress by choosing a good chair. Let's face it; your hands and arms aren't the only part of your body that will tire while hooking. To minimize fatigue in those other places, pick a chair that suits your body size. Make sure your feet reach the floor or footstool and that there is some sort of comfortable back support. An adjustable office chair is a great choice, as it will allow you to roll around to the side of your frame, swivel, change the incline of the back and move up or down. ●

Hooking 101

Proddy Sheep, 19" x 22", #6-cut and hand-cut wool with roving and metallic yarn on backing. Designed by Goat Hill Designs. Hooked by Bernice Herron, Huntington Beach, 2005.

Hooking begins with the way the pattern goes on the frame. Since most frames have square corners, make sure the warp and weft lines of the pattern's backing are put on so they run parallel to the sides of the frame.

Patterns need to be stretched taunt, but not overly tight. You are not stringing a harp. However, a stretched pattern with a lot of "give" will slow down hooking, as well as make it very difficult to achieve even loops.

The pattern should look like this when properly put on the frame.

The backing should be in "square" with the frame, not at a diagonal like this example. Diagonal placement will distort the pattern lines, as well as your hooking. If the pattern is round, use the threads of the backing to determine what is "square."

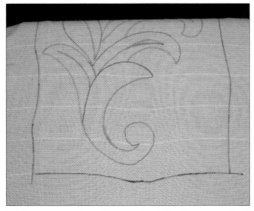

This pattern has been stretched so much that the lines are distorted.

■ **Holding Your Hook**—Experiment with your hook to find the most comfortable way to hold it. There are almost as many ways to hold hooks as there are rug hookers and here is not just one "right" way. Whatever you choose, the best way to hold the hook is the way that works for you.

Use both hands when you hook—they each have a function to perform. While this may seem obvious, most beginners try to do everything with their writing hand. The "writing" hand manipulates the hook while the "other" hand manipulates the wool.

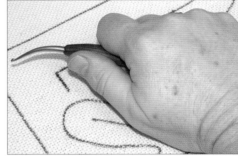

Gene "palms" his bent shaft hook. The ball rests in his palm with the shaft sticking out of his fist at a right angle to the line of his arm. Holding it this way may be a little awkward at first, but it greatly reduces wrist and forearm fatigue and is, therefore, a skill worth learning. Just make sure to never increase the tension in your wrist by gripping the hook in an overly tight fashion—hold it in a loose comfortable way.

Jane holds her straight shaft hook like this, with the ball of the hook nestled between her thumb and forefinger.

1

To begin hooking, insert the hook through one of the fabric's natural "holes" created at the intersection of the warp and weft threads of the backing. Make sure to put the shaft in a hole, not through a strand of backing. Push the hook in up to the wooden shaft and let it sit there until the other hand does its work with the wool. Do not start digging around with the hook trying to find the wool.

2

The whole shaft needs to stick out on the underneath side of the pattern. The more shaft that is under the pattern, the easier it will be to connect with the wool. At this point, your writing hand has stopped.

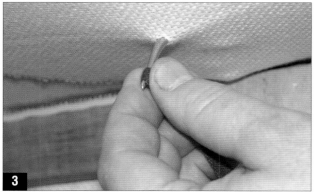

3

Activate the wool hand and use it to place the strip of wool on top of the shaft. Pinch the wool strip "around" shaft so the wool cannot fall off the hook.

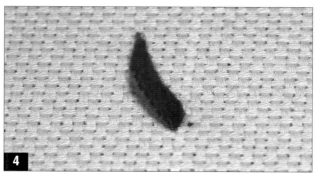

4

Reactivate your hook hand to pull the loop of wool through the hole. The loose end or "tail" needs to stick out enough on the top so that it can't easily work back out. Beginners should leave 1" tails. After a little practice, start leaving ones that are just long enough to stay in. Don't waste good wool by leaving long tails.

■ **The First Loop**—To make the first loop, stick the hook in the next hole. Remember, your hook hand puts the hook in all the way to the wooden shaft and stops. Once there, your wool hand, under the fabric, will loop the wool strip over the shaft as before and pinch it slightly so that it will not fall off the shaft.

Be generous with the wool on this underside procedure. Enough extra length is needed to go around the shaft, provide enough slack for you to hold and then extra to pull through.

■ **Lay It Flat**—Hold the strip of wool flat in your fingers and always lay it flat against the hook in the same way. This is a discipline every hooker needs to learn. Twisted wool makes for bumpy spots on the backside of the rug. Bumpy spots will wear out first as the rug is used. No twisting, no bumps, smooth backside, good job!

■ **Move It Away**—Move the hook away from yourself as you pull the loop high enough to bring the wool up snug against the underneath side of the backing.

This technique corrects three perennial problems that new hookers face; loops on the backside as well as on the top, pulling out the last loop made when pulling the new one, and the inability to make all the loops the same size.

■ **Problem One**—Loops on the backside—Never completely let the wool slip from your wool hand fingers on the underneath side. This keeps the wool strip straight. The wool hand can also feel if the underneath side is properly "snuggled" up to the backing. When you over pull it naturally takes out the slack. We want the loops on the top, not on the bottom!

■ **Problem Two**—Pulling out the last loop when making a new one—Beginning rug hookers often are frustrated to find that after exerting enough pressure to snug things up on the back, the last loop or two hooked has also pulled out. That happens because they pulled the wool towards themselves instead of pulling it away from themselves when bringing up the loop. It may take a little practice to get this technique down, so don't get discouraged. After the first five hundred thousand loops it's really easy!

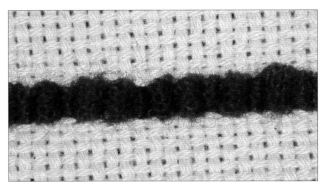

This is how the backside should look. It should be flat, with no loops or tails sticking out. Some of the skips will be slightly longer than others since it requires more wool to go over a skip than it does for neighboring holes.

■ **Problem Three**—The inability to make loops all the same size—At this stage, when the loop is properly pulled, it will snug the wool against the bottom and the loop will be about one-inch high above the topside of the canvas.

Your loop should initially look like this, before you adjust.

This technique of over pulling then adjusting back down to match the existing loops, allows perfect height adjustment every time. It also greatly increases the chance that the underneath side of the rug will have no protruding loops. It does take some extra effort to over pull and then adjust. But this effort is worthwhile as it usually guarantees better-formed loops and a cleaner underneath side. And, once learned, most people go just as fast as anyone else. Some people can hook just the right amount of wool on the underneath side and bring it to the top with out adjusting. If you can do that, more power to you. However, particularly

Keeping the hook in the loop so it can't pull out, use your wool hand to carefully pull the strip from the bottom until the loop is the desired height on the top.

on wider cuts, that procedure does not bring the wool out of the hole enough for the loop to spread out properly. Should you discover a different technique that allows you to achieve a good finished result then, by all means, use that method. However, I have found this to be the simplest way to correct these three perennial problems.

The Proper Height

And the proper loop height would be? That's a matter of both taste and good technique. The loop should be high enough to completely clear the backing and spread out to its full width. If the loops are not well out of their hole and fully formed, or if they are so low that the backing shows through, then you are hooking too low. The old rule of thumb is that the loop ought to be at least as high as the cut width being used. That would make a #8 loop $1/4$" high. An extremely narrow cut, like a #3 or #4, is an exception and should be hooked a little higher than it is wide. There has to be enough height to insure that the loop cannot work back out of its hole. Most artists naturally gravitate to a height that is comfortable to them. In the end, there are high hookers and low hookers, all of whom make equally fine rugs. The goal is to produce a well-constructed rug with a flat and even surface that conceals the backing.

What's Next?

You are now ready for the next loop. Patterns, unfortunately, don't come with directions as to precisely which hole it should go in. Here are a few general guidelines:

■ When hooking a new row, pull two or three loops in succession before skipping a hole.

■ Don't put a loop in every hole. This creates too much pressure on the backing and causes the rug to bubble. It will also eventually weaken the rug. To skip a hole, pull the loop from the second hole over from the last loop, instead of in the hole nearest that loop.

■ Skipping over holes must vary from cut size to cut size. Fine cuts allow less skipping—maybe three or four loops and one skip, etc. When using a wider cut, #5-7, you can usually hook two holes in a row and then skip one—two loops, one skip, two loops, one skip, etc. On bigger cuts you might skip every other hole for two or three loops, before hooking two loops in a row. These directions are meant to be guidelines, not a rigid mandate.

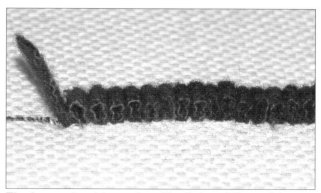

The loops should stand up like little soldiers all in a row. They should just barely touch, not be crowded and pushed out of line.

■ Let your eye guide you in the creation of an even looking row.

■ Since some wool is thicker than others this can also necessitate adjustment. Holes need to be skipped more often for "fat" wool and less for "thin" wool.

Common Frustrations

As other rows are added in, unhooked holes will become invisible. If unhooked holes can be seen after several adjacent rows have been added, then you have skipped too much. However, most hookers are guilty of skipping too little, rather than skipping too much.

The other common frustration for beginning hookers is that their loops lay every which way, not in nice neat regimented rows. Inconsistent hook direction is what causes this.

This hook is positioned to show the direction it pointed when this particular loop was pulled. For such a rounded line, the hook shaft had to function like the minute hand of the clock as it rotated a few "minutes" for every single loop.

Loops lay in the same direction that the hook is pointed. To hook a straight row of loops, your hook always needs to be pointed at a right angle to that line, for every single loop that is pulled.

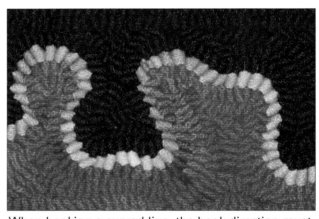

When hooking a curved line, the hook direction must be adjusted for almost every loop. Always hold the hook so that it points across the directional line at a right angle to the spot of that loop. A line like this blue one, demands constant subtle changes in the direction the hook is pointed throughout the entire length of the line.

When the hook direction is changed, it will also change the direction the loop will lay.

By pointing the hook in yet a third direction, you can see that the loops are now laying three different directions. It makes the line look wavy.

At the end of the wool strip or design element, bring the end or "tail" up and let it stick out as you did when starting.

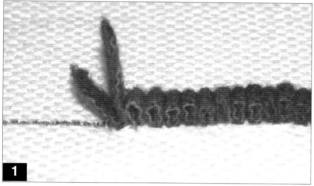

Starting and stopping is the best thing about rug hooking! There are no tails on the backside, no knotting, sewing together of strips, or any other fussy procedures. New strips are spliced in by bringing up the new tail in the same hole where the old one ended.

After hooking a few loops of the new strip, go back and cut off the protruding tails. Carefully lay your bent handled flat scissors on top on the neighboring loops and snip!

Once properly cut, the two ends blend in with the loops and become invisible.

Hooking Direction

Most people find that it is easier to hook from top to bottom. Right-handed hookers usually like to hook right to left and left handed hookers usually like to hook left to right. The person who finds it easier to do it exactly opposite should not despair. You need to find the way that works best for you. No one will give you extra points for hooking in a direction that is awkward for you. Learn your preferences and exploit them to your advantage. If your frame is such that it can be rotated to your advantage while hooking, then do it. Why work harder when you can work smarter? If your frame is stationary, take the pattern off and reposition difficult sections so they are easier to hook.

A row that is square with the backing will run in the "ditch."

Should the ditch be hard to see, open it up a bit by running the backside of the hook's point down the ditch's length. This tends to separate the fibers a bit and open up the holes so they are easier to see. Some hookers use a lead pencil for this.

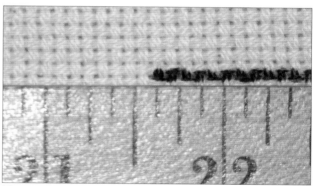

These ditches are the natural perpendicular lines of holes created by the warp and weft threads of the backing. A straight line will be produced when all the holes are pulled in that ditch. If your hook strays outside that ditch, the row will waver. Following the ditch is crucial for the outside border of your rug, if it is to be square.

Bending The Backing

Hooked diagonal rows, unless they are at a perfect 45 degree angle to the backing's warp and weft fibers, are just plain hard to get "right." The backing, because of the way it is woven with North/South and East/West fibers, produces holes in a square grid, much like the old dot matrix printers. This means that all curved lines, shapes, or straight lines not at a right angle must be achieved on a canvas that does not naturally provide holes in exactly the right places. We, therefore, have to bend the backing to our will. Here are a few tips to help with this challenge:

■ First and foremost, point your hook at a right angle to the diagonal line at the spot being hooked. Do not vary. Loop direction is critical to the over all appearance.

■ Don't be surprised that it takes an odd formula of hole skips to hook a diagonal row. Occasionally, you can pull two or three loops in the next diagonal hole. More often than not, it's more like moving chess pieces. You may need to count over one hole, then move down two more holes to find the right place for the next loop. There probably won't be any other repetitive formula than what looks right to your eye. Hook the best line that you can.

■ What is hooked on either side of your initial row is equally important and makes the final determination of how well the row will look. As rows are hooked on either side of the diago-nal, use the new loops to either hold your design line or push it into a better shape. This is one time when it is good to crowd. What holds true for rows also holds true for shapes.

■ If the diagonal row still doesn't look as good as you would like, try removing it and then re-hooking. Often, after the rows have been filled in on either side of your line, you can quickly re-hook something, and it will go in better the second time.

Turning Corners

Turning a corner can be done in three ways. Each has its application. Remember, when hooking any line, you must always consistently point your hook at a right angle to that line.

■ **Skinny Corners**—Skinny corners happen, particularly with wider cuts. Sometimes, crowding before turning the corner is not enough to properly fill in the corner space and make a solid right angle. When this occurs, keep making loops one hole past the corner (that's right, go outside the line) and then make the turn, picking up the new hole back on the ditch of your line. It's just enough to square things up so they look right. You can do this for every corner except for those on the outside edge of your rug. When those corners don't completely fill out, the whipped wool edge tends to cover up so that it is not noticed.

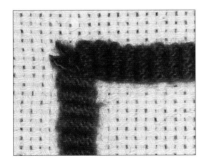

Mitered Corner— The first row is hooked its proper length. With all methods of making corners, it's good to hook the last three or four holes before a corner, with no skips. The tail is brought up in the very corner hole. The perpendicular line is also started with a tail in that same hole. Both tails are clipped after a few loops in the new row have been made.

Repetition of this process for several rows will produce an attractive corner. It does necessitate a lot of cutting. Since it is important that tails begin and end precisely on the mitered line, you may want to actually draw in such a line before you begin to hook. This method is good for backgrounds.

Stop and Start Corner—Hook the row its desired length. The last three or four holes before the end of the row should be filled with no skips. Crowding here is important as it is needed to make the corners look square. Pull the tail and clip. The second row, which will create the right angle, should start butted up against the first row and then proceed as before. The wider the cut, the better it is to use this technique.

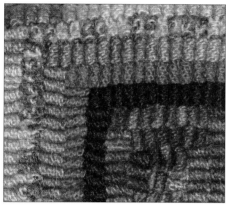

Corner Turn—This is a great method for those who do not like to cut any more than absolutely necessary.

Hook the row to the spot where the right angle turn is to be made. As always, make sure to point the hook at a right angle to that line. The last three or four holes before that corner spot are all filled with no skips. The last loop must be crowded over, instead of standing up straight. Do not cut. Do not bring up the tail.

After hooking the last hole for the first row, turn the hook a 90 degree angle, so that it now points perpendicularly across the new line. Skip the first hole of the new line. Using the same wool strip that is under the frame, bring up the first loop in the second hole and continue hooking. Just changing the angle of the hook will completely change the direction of the loops in the new row.

Hook about three or four holes with no skips before going back to your usual skip rotation. For #3-8 cuts, this is my preferred method of turning corners. It is also my preferred method, regardless of the cut size, when turning corners on the outside row of a square rug. It does leave just a bit of extra wool on the underneath side of the rug, but that is not a problem for #8 on down.

Ending Rows

Ending a row of hooking can be done in a number of ways. The easiest way to end a section or color is to simply bring up the end and cut off the tail. However, when several adjacent rows need to end or begin with tails all on the same line, that straightforward approach would be noticeable.

■ **Staggering**—Staggering allows us to put tails in a place different than the beginning or end or a row. Without doing this, several adjacent horizontal rows of hooking could create a noticeable vertical line of tails.

Begin by bringing up the initial tail one hole over (that would be hole #2 in your ditch) from the finished hole, which would be hole #1 in the ditch.

The second loop will need to be pulled through hole #3. That means, on the underneath side, the wool strip will cross from the first loop over the tail to hole #3, where it will be pulled. While "crossovers" are usually discouraged, it has to be done for this procedure. The topside will have two loops with a tail sandwiched in between. When hooking an adjacent row, start at the normal #1 hole and leave a tail. The third adjacent strip would need to be staggered as described, etc.

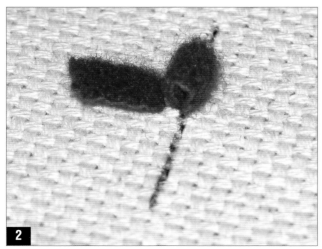

Bring up the first loop in hole #1.

After hooking a few loops you can cut off the tail.

5 If you need to stagger the tail at the beginning of a hooked line, you may also need to do this at the other end. For this, you will make your last regular loop two holes away from where you want your final loop to be.

6 Bring the tail of your wool strip up in the next to last hole of your line. It should look like this on the top-side of your pattern. Do not cut yet.

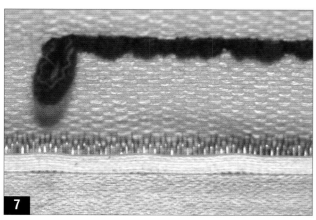

7 The underneath side of the canvas should look like this. The loop on the bottom side should be about inch long.

8 From the top side, stick the hook in the last hole and pull the loop on the underside to the top. Put the hook through the loop so it cannot be pulled out and tug on the tail to adjust loop height. The first adjacent row could end normally, with a tail in the last hole. The third row would need to staggered, etc.

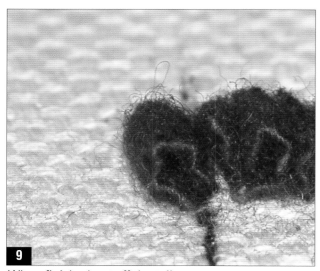

9 When finished cut off the tail.

■ **Hiding An End**—You can completely hide an end, if you want to go to all the trouble it takes to do so.

■ Tails can be left on the backside if your project is a pillow or a wall hanging. Something that has a protective back or will never be on the floor is not adversely affected by hanging tails on the backside. Instead of pulling them through and cutting on top, you just leave them dangling out the backside.

■ Tail tweaking is also an option. Sometimes a plain, square-cut tail end seems a bit too much, even though it's not that big. This is especially true for the end of a vein, or something that ought not to be square. You can lessen the squared off appearance, after cutting off the tail straight in the normal fashion, by going back and cutting off one or both corners of the tail at a right angle. It will make a subtle difference.

■ Personal taste is the final word on tail visibility. Some people hide every single tail. Others always pull every tail to the top. Of those artists, some will work hard to stagger the tails while others will leave them anywhere. Everyone has a rationale for why they do what they do. There really isn't a right or a wrong way as long as it does not compromise the way the piece will be used. While some methods may produce results that are more noticeable than others, one has to get very close to even see the difference. When a piece is completely hooked and on the floor or the wall, the viewer is rarely struck by the tails one may or may not see.

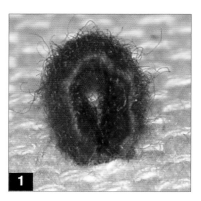

Instead of bringing up the tail end, as one normally would, just bring up a loop.

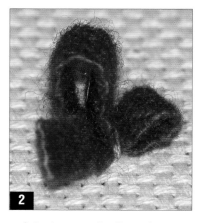

In the next hole over from the loop you just made, pull a loop, making sure to bring up both the strip of wool you are using to hook and the tail. This needs to be done in such a way that the tail comes up inside the loop. Pull the excess part of the tail so that it sticks out of the loop and adjust the height. Continue hooking a few more loops.

Carefully cut the tail end just enough so that you can push it back inside the loop, where it will stay "wrapped up" and out of sight.

Hiding on the other end is a little tricky. Two holes before you want to pull the last loop, bring your wool strip up as though it were one long ending tail.

5

Skip the next hole. In the second or last hole, stick up your hook from the underneath side and pull your wool tail back down, leaving a large loop on the top side.

6

Back on the topside, stick your hook through the hole that was skipped—the one under the large loop. Bring the wool tail through from the backside.

7

Once everything is adjusted, you can cut the tail and poke it inside that last loop where it will stay concealed.

Row Relationships

■ Once a row is hooked, another row has to be hooked next to it. Rows relate to one another in the same way that loops relate to one another. Just as loops in a row should be able to stand up straight, fully expanded, barely touching each other within their row, so too should rows be able to stand up fully formed without being pushed around by other rows. With finer cuts, rows are often hooked in each ditch. However, if the loops begin to look crowded, skip a ditch between rows. In wider cuts, skip at least one ditch between every hooked row. Some cuts require skipping two or three ditches.

There is also a "fluffy factor" in the way that rows relate to each other. This is caused by the different types of wool we use. Some wool tends to be thinner and some tends to be thicker and fluffier. Rows of thin wool will need to be hooked a little closer to the next row than if the wool is "fluffier." Remember that the goal is to put in the least amount of wool, yet cover the backing so that it cannot be seen. Let your eye guide you in this area.

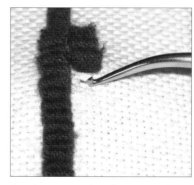

Leave just enough space between rows so that the loops barely touch. In straight row hooking, find the correct ditch and stay in it. If you are hooking a curving line, just do the best you can to place your loops at holes equidistant from the row next to which you are hooking.

A good way to evaluate one's technique is to examine the back side of a rug. If no backing can be seen at all, then there is not enough space between rows. If wide sections of backing can be seen, then too much space is being left. This artist did a perfect job!

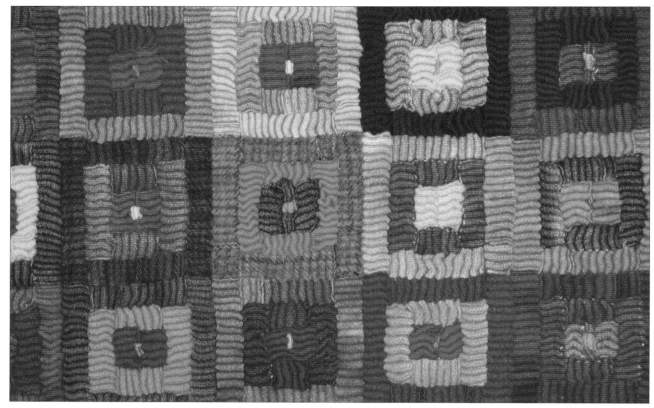

Detail, **My Color Box,** #10-cut with wool selvages. Designed and hooked by Gene Shepherd.

Hooking Shapes

Hooking shapes is just like Coloring Book #101—always stay inside the lines. If loops are pulled right on the design line, the finished project will actually appear bigger than the original drawing. Hooking inside the lines contains the wool loops within the shape, thereby reflecting the lines of the pattern. Properly done, when finished, one ought to be able to pry back the loops and always find the lines of the pattern visible between the various rows of the rug. The only exception to this rule is when a line is the shape you are trying to do, like the vein in a leaf. Then, you do have to hook right on the line.

How far inside the lines does one start? That depends on cut size. Smaller cuts like #3-5 can usually start the first row over from the line of the shape. Wider cuts may need to start two rows over, or even three in the case of some #10s. To find out, hook a few loops and see. Once it is hooked, the fully extended loop will stretch over the hole out of which it comes. Pay attention to where it's "shoulder" sits. If it extends past the line of the pattern or doesn't reach the line, you need to move over another row so that it perfectly fills in the space.

When hooking shapes, all adjacent rows need to reflect the shape you wish to create. This echoing of the shape will help your work to look more realistic. When filling in

an apple, hook successive curving rows the shape of the apple. Don't fill in the shape with straight rows—apples are curved, not straight.

Hooking Squares

There are two basic ways to hook a square shape. Each has its application.

■ **Square Number One—A Block with Personality:** Hook an outline of the square within the drawn shape of the pattern. Go all the way around and stop in the same hole where you started. (Turn corners with your choice of method.) Cut the tails and then proceed inward to where the next row should be. Pick a different place to begin the second row so as not to leave line of tails as you work to the center.

Keep doing this until the shape has been filled. If you want to give the illusion of depth, start with a light shade on the first row and use increasingly darker shades as you proceed to the center. By reversing the shades, the square will appear to be projecting outward. Mixing the colors will produce a totally different sort of square. This technique produces a square where rows of loops are pushing in two different directions. With cuts #3-6, it doesn't seem to matter all that much. However, with cuts #7 and up it tends to make the sides of the square a little rounded.

■ Square Number Two—A Solid Color Square

The second way to hook a square is to outline the square shape within the drawn line of the pattern as before. Starting on one side or the other, fill in with adjacent rows all hooked the same direction. Do not stagger ends, even though all the tails will line up. Some people are so precise that they even repeat the same number of loops in each row to ensure uniform squares. This approach works particularly well for solid squares, like in a checkerboard pattern. There seems to be less "rounding" of the outside with this method.

When doing a checkerboard, think of it as one big design item, not several squares.

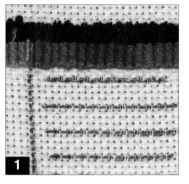

Hook all of the horizontal lines first. Determine the right horizontal ditch to hook in and bring up the first tail right where that row intersects with one of the square's vertical sides. Hook three or four loops without a skip. Proceed in the horizontal ditch until the last tail right is pulled in the vertical ditch separating the two squares. Don't skip any holes for the three or four holes right before this ditch. Change colors and bring the tail up in the same hole as you ended, right in the vertical ditch.

Hook all the top and bottom vertical lines in this fashion. Make sure you start each new horizontal row in the same place. If it is one ditch away from the horizontal design line, do them all one ditch away from each horizontal design line. The entire square could be filled in completely with horizontal rows. However, such a square is not as sharp as one that is outlined.

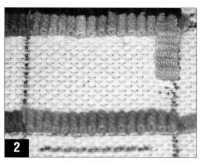

Although the horizontal lines started and stopped right in the vertical line ditch, the vertical rows will be hooked next to the vertical ditch, never in it. The shoulders of the two colors will meet right over that ditch. Due to differences in cut size, you will have to experiment to determine the best ditch to use. Start with the tail butted up against the horizontal line in such a way that the right angle you create is crisp and full.

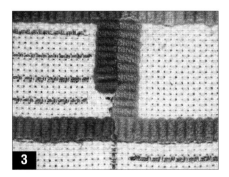

If you hook the vertical row one ditch over from the vertical design line on the green side, you will need to do the same for the red side. Once determined, hook all the vertical rows.

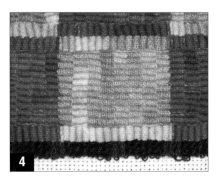

Once the horizontal and vertical lines are all in, it's a simple matter of filling in. Hook one square to see how it fills in with the cut size being used. I was lucky in that eight pieces of my wool perfectly filled the square. However, it's more likely that after putting in so many pieces of one's cut wool, an odd little space will be left—one that is too small for the cut size being used. Since all the squares are exactly alike, this is not a problem. Find out what size that odd piece is. If you are using a #7 and five pieces of #7 fill everything but an odd space the size of a #5, then cut some #5s. Hook each square exactly alike. Always use your combination of #7s and #5s as discussed. If the space is the size of a #5, don't force in a #7. It will distort the square. Take the time to do it right.

Jane always cuts at the point as evidenced by the way she hooks a star.

Hooking Triangles

Triangles can be hooked in either concentric rows or outlined and filled, just as would be done for squares. They are more difficult since two of the sides will be diagonal lines. They are also more difficult because they have "points." Points can be achieved by either cutting at the point or hooking the point.

■ Bring up a tail in the point, and then hook away from that tail in the outline of the star until you get to the next point. In that point, cut and leave a tail.

■ To continue, start the next strip opposite the last loop that was made before the tail, not in the place with the last tail like usual. Continue hooking the outline to the next point. Again, cut your wool and leave a tail in the point.

■ Continue hooking as before, by bringing up the tail next

to the last loop that was pulled. Continue until you have gone the perimeter of the star.

■ Fill in by the same method.

Points can also be hooked without cutting. When leading up to the point, whether it is a straight line as with a star or curved, like in a leaf, hook the last three or four holes leading up to the point with no skips. After the "last loop," skip a hole and bring up the "point" loop in the exact spot where the point is to be. As you do this, twist or point your hook in the "point" direction. This will make the loop stand out at an odd angle. After the point loop, turn the hook so that it is positioned appropriately for the direction of the new row. Bring up the first loop of that new line in the hole below the point loop.

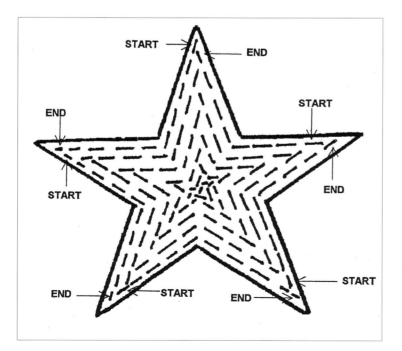

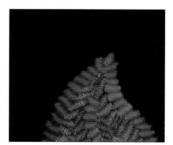

When done properly, the point loop sticks out as a bridge between the two lines of your shape. It doesn't really belong to either line, just points out between them.

Hooking Circles

Circles need to be hooked from the center out. Either "eyeball" or measure to find the center point of your circle. While that center hole will not have a loop, it is an important "rivet" spot that will affect your circle.

Some designs, like "cat's paws," call for an irregular round shape. The circle is begun in the same way as described. However, at any row after the first one, add on one or more "growths" to purposely disfigure your shape. Once done, it foundationally changes the design and affects everything that comes after it.

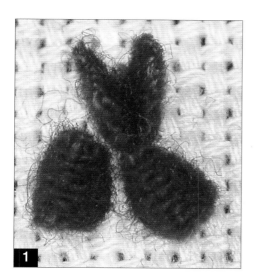

Step 1: Use the center hole as the unfilled center of a three-point triangle—two of the "points" around it will be loops and the third will be a hole containing the beginning and ending tails. Think of the center hole as the spot where a clock hand is riveted to the clock face. Make the three points at "12", "4", and "8 o'clock." Just as the clock hand always points rigidly out from the center, your hook needs to point from the center in exactly the same way to the 12, 4, and 8 spot. Start at 12 o'clock and bring up a tail. Go to the 4 o'clock spot, again, making sure the hook is pointed exactly like a clock hand, and bring up the first loop. Do the same thing at 8 o'clock and then bring up the final tail back at 12. It doesn't make any difference if you point your hook out from the center or in to the center, just as long as the hook shaft mirrors the way a clock hand goes around its face.

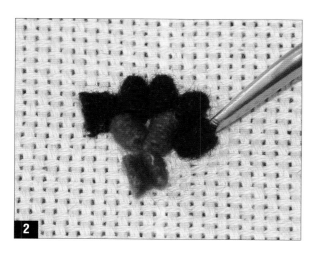

Step 2: Step two in circle making is to corral the center triangle with a circular fence. Pick a spot on the triangle perimeter not next to the tails of the center triangle. It is always good to avoid clustering sections of tails in the same spot if possible. With hook riveted to the center point in clock hand fashion (either pointing in to it or out from it) start making loops around the triangle. Try to make this circle as round as possible. When hooking next to the two initial points, choose the hole closest to the point in order to crowd or nudge it over a bit. This will help produce a rounder shape.

Step 3: This is one of those times when your eye must guide you. If the circle does not look round, take out the loop and redo it. When hooking next to a section that wants to bulge out of line, pull a loop right next to that bulge and force it back into shape. Where you pull the loop and how you point your hook determines the roundness of your design. It's usually best to crowd this first circle a bit, compared to the other successive circles that will follow. Be very particular about this first circle as it lays the foundation for all the others that will come after it. End this circular row by bringing the ending tail up in the same hole where you began.

Step 4: Step four is to keep going around as many times as needed to get a circle the size you want. The second row may also need a bit of crowding here and there to fix the shape. However, by the third row, you ought to have hit a pace that doesn't call for crowding. As before, when hooking next to a previous section that wants to bulge out, force it over with a well placed loop. Don't tolerate rogue loops. Circles hooked in this fashion often want to stick up or out a bit. Don't worry; they will press down when blocked during the finishing process.

Hooking Irregular Shapes

Most of hooking deals with the filling in of irregular shapes. Some shapes work better with an outline and fill technique. Others necessitate that you start in the center and work out. At all times, hook in the direction of your shape's natural contours.

Square Pegs in Round Holes

A properly hooked row, particularly for wider cuts, is very rectangular in appearance. However, when filling in shapes, we often need to fill a space that looks more like a wedge. You can manipulate your strip of wool to do a variety of things that do not look rectangular.

■ You do not have to start your strip in a hole with another tail. A well-placed singular tail will fill a tiny odd space. It will not fall out.

■ Point your hook almost parallel with the line as you pull the loops. This will cause the loop to lay into the space at a different angle, just the way people turn sideways in an elevator to make more room for other people. This is one of those times when you do not want your loop to sit at a right angle to the imaginary line of your space.

■ Gradual change of hook direction in successive loops

will cause your loops to rotate and fill a space that is getting wider. **[See Fingering.]**

■ If a spot is too big to be filled by one tail and too narrow to be filled by one loop, pull a loop up a little high and continue hooking. Go back and cut off the high loop. Two tails take up less space than one loop.

■ When the spot cannot be filled to good effect with the cut size you are using, hand cut a smaller piece that will fit. This often happens with wider cuts.

■ Learn to trust your eye. If it looks like you have forced too many rows in a spot, or that you have distorted your design, chances are your eye is correct. Hooking is not a contest to see how much wool can be crammed into one rug. The goal is to put in just the right amount of wool, in just the right way, so as to make an evenly filled, flat, and finely detailed rug.

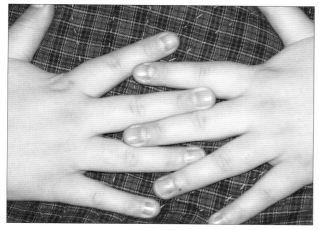

Fingering is achieved when wedged shape rows intersect with each other, much like the fingers of your two hands intersect with one another. A "finger" occurs when hook direction gradually rotates from a right angle position to one that is parallel. It takes about four or five loops to do this. The resultant finger will be wedge shaped.

Fingering

Fingering is a special technique that can be used to either fill in an irregular shape or blend colors of wool.

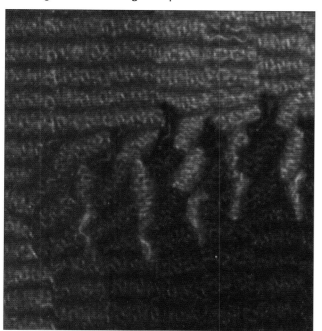

This photo shows how opposing rows can finger in together. Again, the technique is helpful when you have odd wedge shapes to fill. However, its primary use is for blending different colors of wool. The example uses the six values of a swatch. Coming from the right, values are paired with each other as follows: #1 and #6, #2 and #5, and #3 and #4. The closest values really blend together.

The "C" section at the base of this scroll was hooked with a fingered swatch to approximate the effect of a dip dye. Fingering also provides a way to gradually mix different colors of wool. It's often used for fruit.

Maine Coast Scene, 36" x 32", #3- and 4-cut wool on homespun. Designed and hooked by Jacqueline Hansen, Scarborough, Maine, 2002. All of the designs in this border are sculpted. Jackye Hansen regularly creates these wonderful three-dimensional masterpieces.

Sculpted Shapes

Not all rugs are supposed to be flat. There is a whole genre of sculpted rugs known as Waldoboro Style, after the fiber artists of Waldoboro, Maine, who perfected the method in the early part of the 19th century.

Sculpting an entire rug is a big job; however, when done properly, it can be very effective. Before beginning such a project, take note that all regular hooking rules go

Start by hooking an outline row, at regular height, in the shape you want to sculpt. Do not skip any holes. When done, go around the row, carefully inserting your scissors into each loop and cut.

Hook a second row, filing every hole. This time, however, pull the loops so they are a little higher than the first row.

After hooking the second row, go around again and snip the loops. In order to be able to see, periodically use your finger to force the cut loops out of the way.

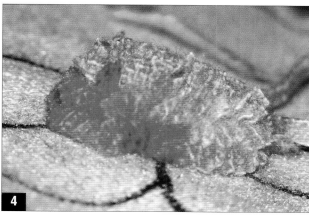

Keep hooking and clipping successively higher rows until the shape is filled. When the shape has been filled in, the wool will stair step up to the highest point in the center.

The sculpting part takes place after all the holes have been filled in and clipped. Take the pattern off the frame and use scissors to shirr off the stair steps, creating a smooth surface. It is best to do this outside! A net brush to whisk away all the lint and fluff is a must for this.

A traditional Waldoboro background is "shirred." To shirr, hook the background any height. However, each hole must have a loop and every loop is cut. It looks like a beautiful piece of velvet when correctly done with a #3 or #4-cut of wool.

out the window when it comes time to sculpt. This method requires a loop in every hole. Loop regularity is not overly important since all of them are cut off. It also uses about two or three times the wool normally needed for a project. While sculpting can be done with almost any size of cut, #3 and #4 cuts produce the smoothest look.

Star Pillow, 14" square, #10-cut of wool on burlap. Hooked by Gene Shepherd, Anaheim, California.

Proddy

Another way to bring a three-dimensional look to your piece is by the method known as "proddy." Based on a form of rug hooking from England, also known as "clippie," both tails from 2" long pieces of wide cut wool are brought through your backing to stick out in shag-carpet fashion.

For traditional proddy, a pattern must be stretched in a rigid frame, like a quilt. The top work area will eventually be the back side of the rug. That requires the pattern to be on the "backside" of the finished piece—just the opposite of rug hooking.

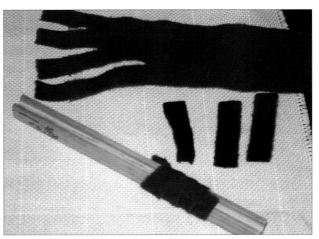

The minimum width for proddy strips is a #10. For pieces this wide, it's not necessary to use a cutter. Measure or eyeball the edge of the wool, cutting little snips every 1/2". Tear into strips. To get 2" pieces, layer the torn wool on a mat and cut with a rotary cutter. A proddy measuring tool makes for even quicker work. After wrapping the strips around the form, a grove allows for an easy scissor cut.

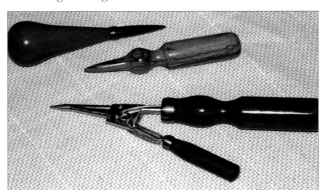

Proddy is usually done with either a blunt smooth shaft that is used to push the wool through from the back or a pincer-like tool that can pull the pieces through the front.

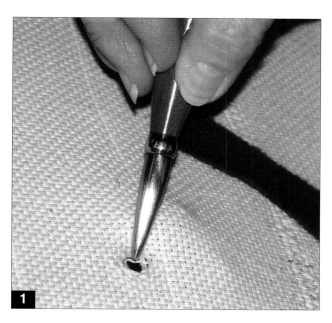

Proddy with a poker—Wool strips are inserted with a poke from the proddy tool. The stick makes a hole, which becomes the home for the first tail. Primitive linen is the best choice for this.

After making the first hole, use the stick to push the tail through. Moving over a row or two, another hole is poked and the other end of the piece is also pushed through. Feel on the underneath side to make sure the tails are sticking out in an even fashion. Tail #1 from piece #2 is inserted in the same hole as the last tail that was prodded. Move over a row or two and make another hole for the second tail. The next piece shares a hole with the last tail poked through and the process is repeated.

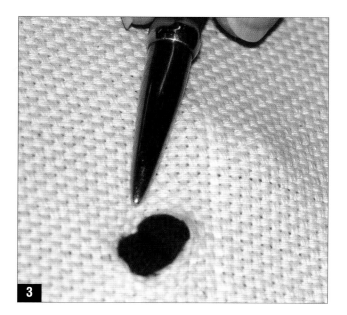

You should always have two tails in each hole. As with hooking, the back should look flat and smooth.

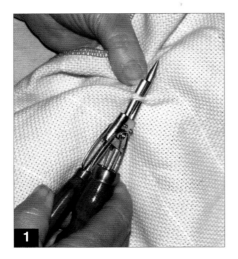

Proddy with a pincer tool—The pincer type tool works from the front instead of the back. Wool pieces are made in the same way as before with two ends sharing one hole. However, this tool pulls each piece through both holes at once. To do so, push the nose of the tool through the spot that is to be the first hole and then bring the nose up a row or two over in what is to be the second hole. Make sure to push the tool in as far as you can up to its hilt.

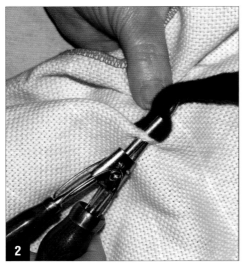

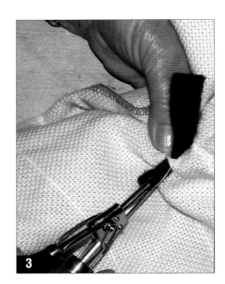

Open the mouth of the pincer and insert a wool end. Close the tool and pull the wool piece through so that it is evenly divided between the two holes.

Start the process again by inserting the nose in one of the existing holes and coming up a row or two over. Open the mouth to receive an end and pull it through and continue. No frame is required for this method. The pattern can be held in your lap as you work from the front.

Additional effects can be achieved by shaping the ends of the 2" pieces. Measure and cut them as before. Then, folding a piece one at a time, cut the end to shape as desired—they can be rounded or pointed, for example, to look more like a flower petal. This effect is good for wall hangings or other places that require some texture.

Multiple Ways to Hook

One of the beautiful things about artistic expression is that there is never just one way of doing things. This chapter seeks to underscore and illustrate that truth by hooking three simple designs in a variety of ways. Even when designs are drawn for fine shaded patterns, they certainly do not have to be hooked that way. We hope to encourage your experimentation with these variations on a theme.

Shaded rug hooking is traditionally done with wool from a "swatch." Traditional fine shading using swatches is really a very simple technique. In this line drawing, the numbers tell the color value to use. Number one is for the lightest value and six is for the darkest. The broken lines show the direction that should be hooked. They are placed in such a way as to show how much of any given value should be used. The letters indicate the order in which the various sections should be hooked.

■ **Cut Size**—Cut size varies for this type of hooking. While we usually think of the finer cuts, such as #3 and 4, when fine shading, the size of the design really dictates the cut that can be used. This particular rose design, with a bloom that is 8 ¹/₂" across at its widest point, was created specifically for a #6-cut, hence the name of the design. Technically, one could do fine shading with a #10 if the design was big enough.

■ **Wool Choices**—Wool choices for traditional fine shading are pretty much limited to value swatches. We use 6-value swatches in this book. However, they do come in sizes with more values. Some swatch colors are coordinated, so that 12 or 18 values can be created by combing two or three swatches.

Six-cut rose

Fine-shaded six-cut rose

Fine-shaded rose, #6-cut wool on backing. Designed by Jane Olson and Gene Shepherd. Hooked by Jane Olson.

A swatch usually has six to eight pieces of wool in varying values of the same color. A red 6-value swatch will have six pieces of wool, each in a different value of the same red. The first piece will be the lightest, the second piece a little darker, with each getting successively darker until you reach the darkest at value 6.

To begin, hook section A. Always start by hooking the sections that seem to sit "on top" of the design. This petal lip does that. Start at the top of the lip with value #1 and hook it down the entire length of the petal lip. Make sure to hold the hook at a right angle to this line as it curves downward. This will help produce a fluid and natural line. The second strip of #1 would start a little lower down from where the first row was hooked. Keep your rows inside the perimeter line of section "A." Values #2 and #3 are added in the same way.

Proceed by going to the next letter, which would be B, then C, etc. Always follow the value chart and always follow the curve of the broken lines. The value sections are not always broken up evenly. That's because light does not necessarily fall on each petal in an even way. As any given section is hooked, it may be difficult to work in all the values. Don't worry as this sort of additional irregularity only helps the finished piece to look more natural. The contrast of light values against dark ones causes different sections of the rose to stand out. That is why the diagram calls for a little extra #6 at the bottom of most petals.

The leaves are shaded on this piece as well. Take note of the fact that they were not all shaded the same way. Some have a light center, shading out to a dark edge. Others have a dark center shading out to a light edge. Still others have half a leaf that is shaded dark to light, with the other half being shaded light to dark. The leaf veins are leftover bits from the flower, in various combinations. All these variations make the piece more interesting, as well as realistic.

Finished fine-shaded rose.

DIP-DYED ROSE

Dip-dyes are great for rug hooking as one piece of wool automatically changes color without the bother of using different pieces. However, this benefit does require a different hooking technique than what would be used for a 6-value swatch.

Dip-dyes are created when a long piece of wool is lowered very slowly into a dye bath. Since the wool takes up more dye the longer it is in the bath, the eventual product is a piece of wool that begins dark and gradually changes to light. In this instance, the ends have also been tipped with a bit of pink. This is different than a 6-value swatch which uses six different pieces of wool to achieve the same color gradation.

Dip-Dyed Rose, #6-cut wool. Hooked by Jane Olson.

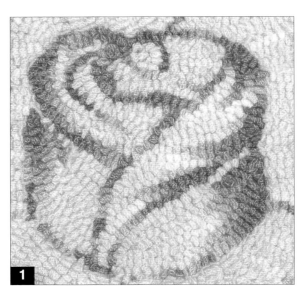

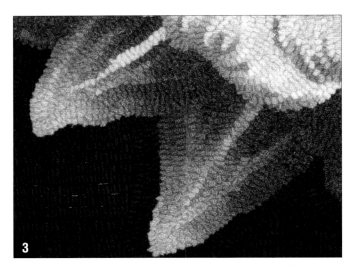

Notice the bud of the dip-dyed rose. When hooking the first value of the swatch on the initial lip of the bud, it was hooked from top to bottom, using any value, or successive values. However, with the dip-dye, hooking must work horizontally in order to get gradation.

The leaves clearly show the value of a dip-dye. One could almost feel guilty using a specialty dye process that looks so good with so little effort. It's not a feeling that lasts very long!

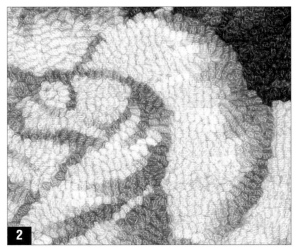

This is more noticeable in the petals. Before, successive values were hooked in the arc shape of the petal. With the dip-dye, hooking begins at the base of the petal and proceeds out to the edge of the lip if that similar gradation is to be achieved. This technique is a little tricky with a rose since it would not look natural to hook straight lines from the base out to the edge of the petal. As can be seen, Jane has a bit of a curve in her hooked line, which makes the petal look more realistic.

Finished **Dip-Dyed Rose Pillow**

SCRAP ROSE

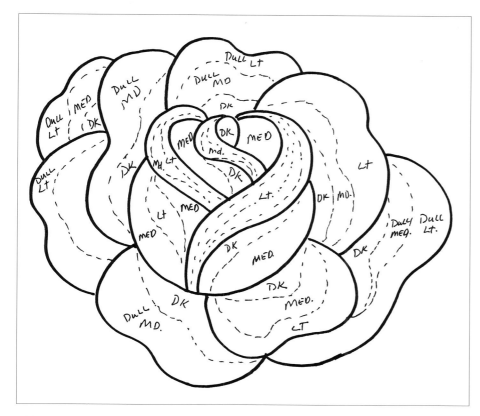

A scrap project results from "making do" with what is on hand at the time you decide to hook. It would be nice if every detail on a rug could be planned and then dyed for every project we do. However, the creative muse doesn't always give that much notice. Then, again some of us are surrounded by so much extra wool, that if we don't start using it we can't buy more the next time we go to rug camp! It really can be rather exciting to just start rooting through one's stash, to see what can be found and used for the project at hand. This type of hooking is certainly not new, as it harkens back to the originators of our art form who were quick to recycle any useable fabric they could find. They often used fabrics together that were nothing more than "close" in color and value. For this particular project, the style is somewhat similar to that of fine shading. You just don't use precise swatches and the cut is medium to wide.

■ **Wool Choices**—If swatches had been used for this piece, there would have only been six to eight wool options of pink, or whatever color that was chosen. That is plenty to do a rose. However, if you really study a pink rose in the garden, you'll notice that there are all sorts of places where a pink rose isn't pink. Sometimes you'll see a blush of coral, yellow or even orange where the petal attaches to the stem. At other places the pink fades into beige or cream. When assembling scraps for this project I ended up

Cut Scrap Rose, #6-cut wool. Hooked by Gene Shepherd.

with about 20 pieces of wool in pinks, corals, and beiges. Frankly, I like breaking up a smooth gradation of one color with other compatible, yet different, colors. Again, it replicates the way real roses look in the garden. Odd pieces of wool can be tested for color compatibility by making a nosegay of "wool flowers" as you sort through your stash. If various colors seem to "work" when put together as a bouquet, they usually will hook up in the same fashion.

■ **Cut Size**—Cut size was limited to #6 throughout this piece. A #8 could have been substituted, however, increasing the width of the cut in this case would give the artist less space to play with color since the petals aren't that big.

■ **Hooking Scraps**—Hooking scraps does not mean that one does not pay attention to fine shading directions. In this case, they provide a wealth of information as to where places on the rose should have dark values and where they should have light ones. As always, start by hooking sections that sit "on top" of the design. In this case it would be the "light lips" that frame the tight center bud.

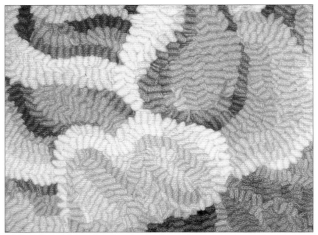

After hooking the bud section, the next step is to move to the bottom petal, since it sits on top of the design. The petals get a little duller as they progress out from the center. These dull lights and darks, many with beige overtones, were used on the outer rows of the petals.

When hooking this style of piece, try doing the following three things :

■ Look at real roses as often as you can, trying to identify the various colors and shades that pop up on or against their petals.

■ Don't be afraid to hook in the different colors you see.

■ Always assess your work at a distance because that's how most people will see it. What looks a little strange up close often blends in effectively when you are on the other side of the room. ●

There are four families of very light wool just in these top lip sections—two different pale pinks, a rose and a dusty pink. To provide vivid definition, deeper values were hooked next to the lips. The center utilizes the brighter and the richer of both the light and dark wools that were used.

Finished Scrap Rose Pillow

OUTLINE AND FILL

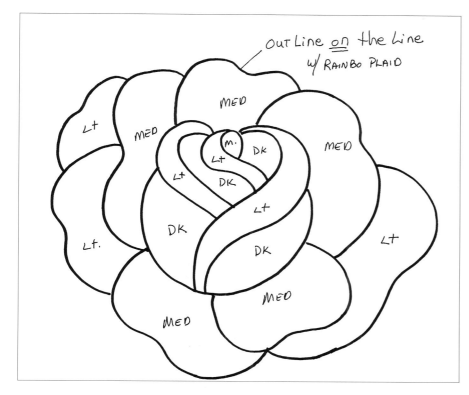

Outline *on* the Line w/ RAINBO PLAID

MED
Lt
MED
MED
m.
DK
Lt
Lt
DK
Lt
Lt.
DK
DK
Lt
MED
MED
MED

Outlining a design with one color of wool, then filling it in with another color, is about as simple a technique as there is. Some people refer to it as the primitive way to make a hooked piece. Such a rigid classification deserves to be broken as evidenced by this style, which can help you create something that is anything but primitive. Outline and fill can be easier and quicker to do than either shaded, dip-dyed, or scrap methods because you have fewer decisions to make while hooking any given section. It's also a technique that seems to work particularly well for wider cuts.

■ **Cut Size**—Although this pattern was intended for a #6-cut, everything but the outline was hooked with a #8. Since the rose itself is only 8" x 7", with several internal parts, #8 was just too thick and heavy for the outline. If the rose had been even 50% bigger, a #8 could have been used effectively all the way through the piece. #6 for the outline was a better choice.

■ **Wool Choices**—With outline and fill, the lines are hooked in one color and fill is hooked with another. However, just a bit of variation provides a lot more personality. When rooting through my stash of wool to make this piece I found some spot-dyed wool, which had never been used.

The outline wool is what really sets off the entire piece. As providence would have it, my stash had a one-yard long piece of checked material, over dyed with rainbow colors. It had been bought a couple of years before on impulse, from Gail Dufresne. The unexpected change in color of the outline material, as it goes around the various

Outline and Fill Rose, #8-cut wool on backing. Hooked by Gene Shepherd.

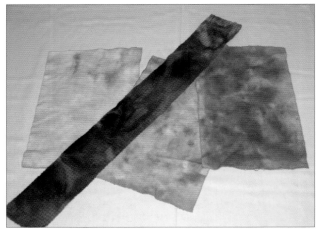

While it was all the same general color, there happened to be a fairly light section, medium section and dark section. Those sections were separated for the project. The darkest and lightest pieces were used for the center bud of the rose. The 5 closest petals outside the center bud were done in the medium wool, with the 3 more outside petals being the lightest wool. This variation of color gives just enough difference to make the piece look much more realistic.

shapes, makes the rose and leaves appear to have all sorts of natural highlights. A piece of mottled wool with strong contrasting colors and highs and lows would also create much the same effect. However, Gail's combination of checks and colors really pays off in the finished piece.

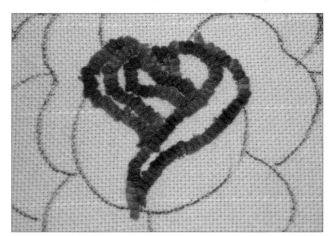

■ **Outlining**—For this particular technique, you need to hook the outline right on the design lines.

That goes against what we have already told you—to always hook inside the lines so as to not distort the shape and size of whatever you are hooking. However, in this instance, the outline wool is just that—outline. It will blend in almost like a shadow. The colored wool is what will give the appearance of the "rose shape" to the piece. All the rose colored wool will be inside of the lines created by the outline wool. The outline is always done first, and then filled in. Since variegated wool was being used for the

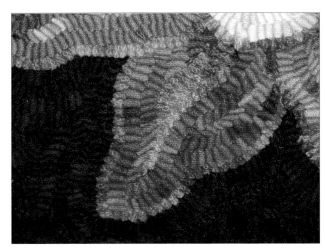

Although this section isn't about leaves, its easy to see that three different pieces of wool were used for the leaves—light green, medium blue green and wine—all mottled. These were all outlined with the rainbow check wool and then filled in.

outline, some attention was paid to where the colors landed—the darker sections being used where a little more shadow was wanted and lighter colors where a little more sparkle was wanted.

■ **Filling In**—Each rose petal has its own shape and it is important to hook in the direction of that shape so as to make the petal look as realistic as possible. To do this, start at an outside edge and hook next to the outline wool. This is done in successive rows until the entire space of one petal has been filled.

Start in the center of the rose since that is the section that sits on top of the design. After outlining the three light colored petal turnovers, they should be filled in before moving on to the darker bud. After that, proceed to the five medium petals and then finish with the three light outer petals.

Finished Outline and Fill Rose pillow, 18" square.

THE MAPLE LEAF

The maple leaf, particularly in its fall splendor, is one design that just doesn't have a good fine shaded application. After all, there is nothing too precise about the riot of color that is the fall maple leaf. We are fortunate to have at our disposal so many specialty dyes that help us produce such wonderful results. Four basic applications are given for this design. However, we'll be disappointed if you don't experiment and come up with your own ways to interpret this basic shape.

Maple Leaf Pillow, #6-cut wool on monk's cloth. Designed by Jane Olson. Hooked by Jean Coon, Newport Beach, California.

A dip-dye is a piece of wool that has been gradually dipped in dye so as to take up color in a graduated fashion. It allows the artist to achieve with one strip of dip-dye what would otherwise take six strips from a swatch. Of course, the basic formula can be changed by dipping three different pastel wool strips into the dye at the same time, or tipping one end with another color. In fact, one doesn't even have to dip a dip-dye! You can spread the wool out in a pan and pour a strong dye solution on the bottom section, a medium solution on the middle, and weak one on the top. This can be done with one or more colors. The shades will run together and produce the desired gradation. The end result will produce an unbroken color strip with great variation.

■ **Cut Size**—Cut size can vary for this style of hooking. Jane typically prefers smaller cuts and used a #4 for this project. However, larger cuts up to a #8 would also work. As cut size increases though, detail in the leaf edge will lessen. With an even dip dye, all the wool can be cut before hooking starts. A different, appropriate vein color will need to be selected for the leaf. Should a #8-cut be chosen for the leaf, a smaller cut would look better for the vein.

■ **Wool Choices**—Wool choices cease once the decision has been made to use a specific dip dyed piece. Each cut piece will be roughly the same, so it does not make too much difference when

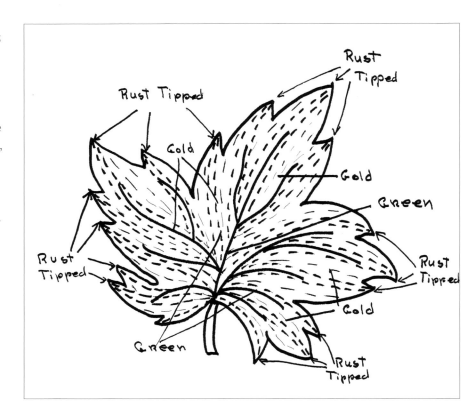

Dip-Dye Leaf, #4-cut wool. Designed and hooked by Jane Olson.

On some of these leaf edges, Jane started with the red tipped end of her wool and hooked in to the vein. As she worked down the edge of the leaf, she began to start hooking on her strip at a point below the reddish tip. She changed the color of the leaf edge by varying where on the strip she started hooking. That means there was a bit of waste with those lower, shorter strips of wool. However, the variation was worth the waste.

Detail, **Eastham Moors.** 48" x 72", #8-cut wool on backing. Designed by Lib Callaway. Hooked by Jan Winter, Hollywood, California, 2001. Dip dyes are perfect for nearly any kind of leaf design as evidenced by this wide cut version. On some of these leaves, the artist used two different, yet similar, dip dyes for effect.

each piece is hooked. It does matter where hooking starts on that particular strip and that does give us artistic choice.

■ Begin by hooking the veins. If a realistic leaf is your goal, use a light color of contrasting wool for the veins. Although rug hookers often hook veins in very dark contrasting colors, most real leaves have light veins.

■ Proceed by hooking either from the leaf edge in to the vein or from the vein out to the edge—either way is fine.

■ Do not outline the leaf with the dip dyed wool, because that would spread all the color variations around the edge of the leaf. Careful examination of the photo reveals that Jane sometimes does go along the edge with a loop or two,

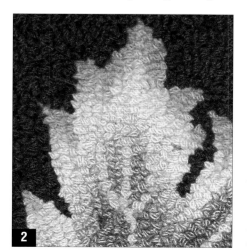

particularly at leaf sections where there is a slender point, before heading down to the vein with the strip. This allows for a smoother edge and still concentrates the colors where they need to be. Let your eye guide you. If something is needed to hook to or from, outline the leaf with a piece of the background before starting.

■ Make sure the rows of leaf strips generally run parallel fashion with each other as they angle down to the vein lines. This will make the leaf look more natural. Given the fact that some of the sections of the leaf will be shorter and others longer, a natural varied gradation will result because those sections will use different amounts of the dip dye piece. Save all left over sections from each strip. If they are long enough, these can be used at other places in the leaf. For example, if you started at the top of the leaf with your lightest section, yet ended in the middle of the gradation at the vein, take the leftover piece and drop down to the bottom part of the leaf. Start there at the vein and hook out to the edge. After all, a maple leaf is usually never perfectly tipped with one color all the way around its edge. ●

If the wool is tipped with just a bit of color that is wanted around the edge of the leaf, then start with the edge and hook in to the vein. That way, the leaf can take advantage of every loop of that color. If the edge doesn't make a difference, hook from the center out. Since a dip dye goes from light to dark, or one color to another, its important to always hook in the same color sequence—either all the light on the edge to a darker center or vice versa.

There are serious cutting issues with this process. The "ordered" part of this technique is the way the strips are hooked. They have to be hooked in the sequence that they are cut. This type of hooking will preserve the shapes of the dye spots on the wool.

Pancake Casserole Leaf, #5-cut wool. Hooked by Gene Shepherd.

Normally, when this method is used, four or five colors are spooned on the wool. To do this, wool piece #1 is placed on the bottom of a casserole pan. A different color of dye is liberally spooned on each of the four corners so that they all run together in the middle. A fifth color can be put in the center. There is nothing rigid about the number of colors that are used, or where they are placed on the wool. As long as the finished piece looks like a splotchy wool leaf, any combination will work. Piece #2 is placed on top of the first and the dye process is repeated until several layers of wool have been "pancaked" in the pan. If both light and dark leaves are wanted, half way through the process the dyes can be diluted with water. That will make the top pieces lighter than the bottom ones. Even the colors can be changed as the stack is created. Once the pan is full, it is covered and placed in a 300° oven for 30 minutes. Make sure there is a little extra water in the bottom of the pan before baking.

Every piece will be a little different as the colors tend to blend more while baking.

Only two colors were used for this piece since a simple, realistic leaf was the goal. Those colors were spooned on in such a way that it produced a rather splotchy dip-dye.

Ordered Pancake Casserole Leaf—Here is another leaf created with this dye method. The wool used had a different color on each corner and another in the middle. By cutting and then sequentially hooking a few pieces at a time, a much more realistic leaf was achieved.

This method of dyeing leaves provides the graduated color changes of a dip-dye, yet can also include the additional random color shift which one finds in real leaves. It's an easy method to do since measuring and exactness does not come into this technique.

Specialty dyed wool for this type of hooking is achieved by cutting several pieces of wool the size of your casserole dye pan. They are layered in one at a time, while two to five colors of dye is spooned over each piece.

Once hooking begins, it should proceed in pretty much the same fashion as that of the dip-dyed leaf. Hook the

veins first. Lighter veins will look more realistic than darker ones. When doing the leaf itself, it's best to hook from the outside edge in to the vein. Hook the leaf colors in generally parallel rows as they angle down to the veins. Leftover pieces that are long enough should be used at other "lobes" of the leaf. Let your eye guide you. Remember, you are painting with wool.

When using this method, cut the wool as it is needed. Make sure the pieces stay in the order they were cut. The piece closest to the cutter guide is piece #1, the next piece in would be #2, the one after that would be #3 and so on. Hook the strips in that numerical order. Do not cut "ahead" of your usage, unless you have some way to tape the pieces down so they do not get out of order. This way, the splotches on the wool will be replicated on the hooked leaf. If the wool gets mixed up, the end result will be a striped leaf, instead of one that has spots. A #5 cut was used for this project.

Do Veins 1st

Fill w/CONTRASTING Values

Scrap Leaf, #8- and 6-cut wool. Hooked by Gene Shepherd.

Leaves are a great way to use up leftover wool. Attractive leaves can be made without a complicated specialty dye process.

■ **Wool Choices**—When assembling potential wool pieces, be sure to pick more colors than you think will be needed. It's also important to have a mix of both plain and textured pieces in your "palette." The more wool pieces used will mean wider variety of color combinations in the various leaves. This is particularly important if you choose a design that has a lot of leaves. Pick something for a vein that will contrast with the colored wool. Although veins in nature are almost always lighter than their host leaf colors, anything can be chosen for this method.

■ **Cut Size**—Cut size can vary from #3-8 with this style of hooking. It seems to work best, however, with cuts #6-8. Although this pattern is only a 6" leaf, a #8-cut was used for everything but a few of the veins, where a #6 was used. Thinner veins generally make for more attractive leaves. If the leaf design was bigger, even the widest cuts could be used for this type of hooking.

Begin by hooking the

veins. Start on the outside tips of the veins and work in or down.

Scrap hooking is a good exercise since it requires the artist to "paint with wool." It's often difficult to judge the success of such paintings until the piece is completely finished. Rug hookers frequently make the mistake of ripping out more wool than they put in. Don't do any reverse hooking until entire leaf has been finished. It's amazing how the appearance of a hooked design can change as the eye starts to "blend" the wool pieces in watercolor fashion. Wool pieces that seemed awful when standing alone on the pattern frequently look just right when surrounded by other rows. When done, make the final judgment by viewing the piece from across the room. If something still offends, that is the time to remove it. ●

Instead of holding the hook at the normal right angle to the vein line, point the hook in the same direction as the line when bringing up the first tail and loop. Then, gradually rotate the hook so that by the third or fourth loop the hook is pointing in a right angle to the vein line. This will produce a pointed vein, instead of a boxy one. It's really important to do this with the wider cuts, as their squared ends are more noticeable than the ends of the finer cuts.

As leaf colors are filled in; hook down to the vein with wedge shaped rows. "Finger" in the various colors, as was discussed in Chapter 2. Use contrasting wool pieces in some sections and similar wool pieces in others. These variations will make the leaf more interesting.

OUTLINE AND FILL LEAF

Outline
EDGE &
Veins 1st

Fill w/ uniform
Rows

Outline and Fill Leaf, #6 cut wool. Hooked by Jean Coon.

Some rug designs are not intended to be overly realistic. We can have "padula" leaves—representational leaves—just like we can have padula flowers. Outline and fill is a great way to interpret such designs, particularly when one wants to do wider cuts.

■ **Cut Size**—Cut size can be anything for this method. However, since it is not particularly subtle, why waste time with anything smaller than the #6 our artist used for this piece? Bigger sizes can also be used, if the design is large enough to handle them. The widest cuts don't work well in small designs. Pick a maneuverable cut size that works with your design. You can drive a bus almost anywhere; however, it's easier to turn it around in a parking lot than it is in your driveway! The same is true for cut sizes.

■ **Wool Choices**—Wool choices for this type of hooking are unlimited. This sort of project is just the ticket for the small or left over pieces most rug hookers end up with because they can't bear to throw away any good wool. Our artist used vivid, multi-colored spot dyes for the outline and vein wool.

To fill, she used complimentary solid, mottled wool.

Hooking begins with the veins and edge outline, which were done with the spot dyes. Once done, it's a matter of filling in with the solid mottled wool. Even though a solid color is being used for the fill, it's still important to hook rows that are roughly parallel to each other as they angle down to the vein lines. Hooking direction gives movement to a finished piece even when the wool is a solid color. Because this piece is mottled, it is even more noticeable.

There are special concerns with this type of hooking. It's true that outline and fill is, comparatively, a simple technique. However, that does not give the artist license to "slide" on their hooking technique. ●

Try these two variations on this design.

1. Continue the use of one spot dye for the edge and vein. When filling the leaf, use a different contrasting color on each side of the leaf.

2. Outline half the leaf with one solid color and fill with another. On the other side of the same leaf, switch positions and do just the opposite with the wool. A third contrasting color or spot dye can be used for the vein.

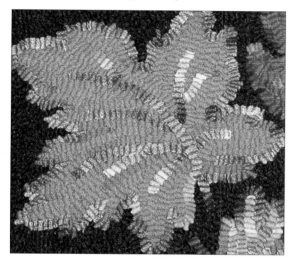

Given its simplicity and the large spots of plain hooking, mistakes are more noticeable, not less. When looking at this leaf, the precision and even loops of the artist really stand out.

You can actually mix different spot dyes with the same fills, all in the same piece, as long as they are all compatible. Go with color choices that look good to your eye.

Since the early 1900s scrolls have been almost the exclusive property of the artists who used fine shaded, and then later, dip-dyed techniques. However, it was not always that way. Many early hooked rugs employed very primitive scroll designs. Sometimes the entire scroll was all one color. Other artists would outline with one color or texture and then fill in with another color or colors. Happily, the scroll is versatile enough for those who wish to include it as either an elegant or primitive design. This particular design is a leaf scroll.

■ **Wool Choices**—Wool choices for this piece are limited to two contrasting 6-value swatches. The purple swatch is used for the base, veins, and topknot of the scroll. The green swatch provides the leaves. The diagram uses numbers to dictate the values used for each section, with #1 being the lightest and #6 the darkest.

Fine Shaded Scroll, #4-cut wool. Designed by Jane Olson and Gene Shepherd. Hooked by Jane Olson.

The diagram is labeled with:
- Lavendar
- outline Dk. Green
- G
- H
- F
- D
- all veins #6 of Lavendar
- E
- C
- shade
- all other scrolls Green
- B
- A
- outline Dk. Green
- Lavendar
- LD Fine SHADED Scroll

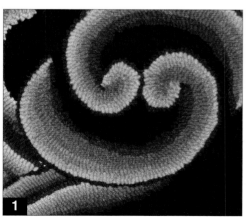

Hooking order is always determined by what sits on top.

In this design, start with the base of the scroll—section A. After that, proceed from section to section as you hook through the alphabet. Everything is very straightforward in this rendition. The base of the scroll is first outlined with the #6 dark green of the swatch. The "fill" is given with for the various values needed.

Proceed to the leaf that sits on top of the others. That would be section B. Value #1 starts at the tip of the scroll and is hooked the entire length of the line back to the internal point at the base. The leaves are divided by the darker values of the contrasting purple swatch. Each side of the leaf uses all six values. The leaves that turn in to the right are hooked from the top arc in, dark to light—vein—dark to light. The leaves which arc to the left are hooked just the opposite—light to dark vein—light to dark.

The "leaf parts" of the scroll are hooked from the outermost tip back to the place where the leaves overlap.

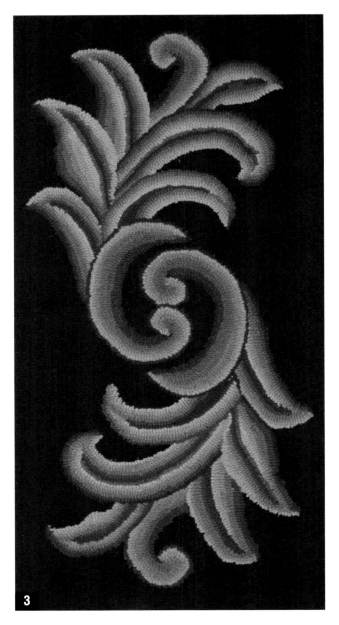

The last section to be hooked is the purple topknot. Like the "C" shaped base, it is outlined with the darkest green and then filled with successive values of the purple.

DIP-DYED SCROLL

The nice thing about a dip-dye is that it does much of the work for the artist! A well-dyed piece of wool will create a wonderful gradation that is naturally suited to the arc of a scroll. No wonder that this is the preferred scroll technique for artists today.

■ Wool Choices—Wool choices were selected from a stash of wool that the artist created specifically for this project. Using formulas from *Scrolls are Easy* as a general guide, Jan Winter experimented with various middle greens (Nile, Mint, and Hunter) as well as other blues and greens (Sky Blue, Myrtle, and Navy) for the ends. She only used new white, natural, and light beige wool for this project. Some of the tips got a light wash of yellow if they were too light. Concerning this process, Jan confesses that she doesn't rely on a lot of stock formulas. "I just mess around until I come up with something that looks okay!" By using various combinations of the same dyes, over different colors of wool, the end results will be related and should therefore be compatible when used together. By her own admission,

Jan dyed more combinations than she ended up using. "I like to have plenty of options from which to choose," she said.

A well-dyed piece of wool will create a wonderful gradation that is naturally suited to the arc of the scroll.

Dip-Dyed Scroll, #6-cut wool. Designed by Jane Olson and Gene Shepherd. Hooked by Jan Winter.

This close up photo clearly shows the different results Jan's dye process produced. There is enough difference to be clearly visible, yet all are related. The "tweed" veins really show up against the plain wool.

Detail, **Rapture,** #4-cut wool. Designed by Jane McGown Flynn. Hooked by Lisa Rueger.

The process of dip-dyeing similar dye baths over different colors of wool also comes in very handy for flowers, like this lily. Five different related dip dyes were used for the various petals. Similar pieces can be created by dipping white, natural, beige, and three or four different pastels all at the same time in the same dye bath.

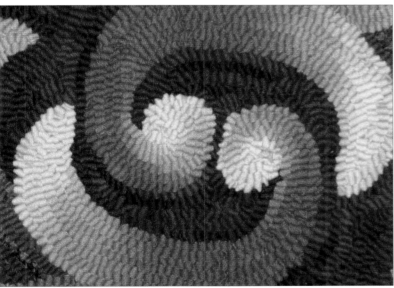

To begin hooking this scroll, start with the section that "sits on top" of the other design elements.

The "C "shape section, at the base of the scroll (labeled A) is the place to begin when hooking this design. Notice the light section at both ends of the C. This can be achieved by hooking a light tipped dip dye piece from each end. Their darker sections will meet in the middle. A special piece of double dip dyed wool can be created for this need and is described under "Bricks" in Chapter 4.

The leaf sections are all hooked with dark wool at the base to a light end tip. Variation is achieved by changing the dip dyes used from leaf to leaf. For different ways of hooking the leaf point see Chapter 2, "Hooking Triangles."

Always remember, the rug's backside should look as neat as the front. Make sure there are no ends sticking out or cross-overs. If none of the backing is visible, not enough space is being left between rows. A lot of visible backing signals that too much space is being left between rows.

Finished **Gene's Scroll,** Dip-dye example. Hooked by Jan Winter.

SCRAP SCROLL

The artist for this example was given the assignment of limiting her wool choices to whatever could be found in her scrap pile. "It was a challenge to use on-hand wool—certainly not as easy as I thought it would be! It makes me think how I will gather wool for my stash in the future," says Annie Wilson. Yet, the finished product is a very pleasing rendition, certainly reminiscent of early hooked rugs.

Starting places and general hooking directions are the same for this scroll as with the others in this section. Even though it is a straightforward design, constant care must still be given to pointing the hook in such a way as to make a natural curved row.

"It was a challenge to use on-hand wool—certainly not as easy as I thought it would be! It makes me think how I will gather wool for my stash in the future." —*Annie Wilson*

Scrap Scroll, #8-cut wool. Hooked by Annie Wilson.

Only four different pieces of textured wool were used for this design. The three green pieces, which are also three different values, were "as is" wool. The red plaid had been over-dyed.

The darkest wool unifies this piece, as it is the only wool used throughout the design. By deliberately staggering the use of the other two green pieces, as well as limiting the appearance of a "red vein," the artist creates more interest. The overall effect is certainly not as elegant as the first two examples. However, more and more artists and collectors are choosing more primitive styles that capture the look of earlier rugs.

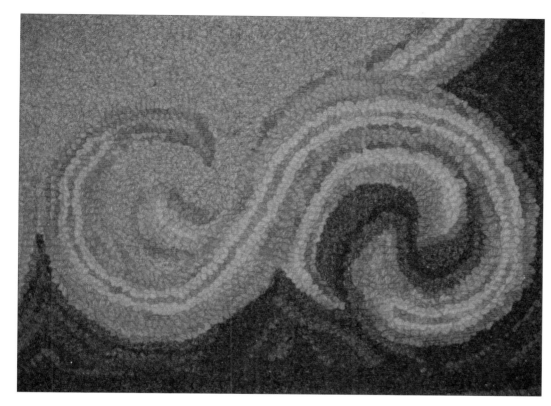

This scroll, from an antique rug in the Marion Wise collection, uses scraps in a way that is both haphazard and effective. No doubt the artist was also using up available wool. Still, the end result works and should be an encouragement for wide cut artists to interpret scroll designs in a variety of simple ways.

Finished **Scrap Scroll,** #8-cut wool on monk's cloth. Hooked by Annie Wilson.

This version of our scroll is about as simple as it gets. Only two colors of mottled wool were used. Each color is used to outline and vein half of the leaves, with the opposite color being used for the fill. All of it is done with a #8-cut. Although very simple, it nonetheless makes a striking design statement which wide-cut artists can incorporate into their designs. It is hooked in roughly the same fashion and order as the other scrolls.

OUTLINE & VEIN IN A

OUTLINE & VEIN IN A

SOLID A

B
B

OUTLINE & VEIN IN A

B

B

B

B

A

A

A

A

A

B

B.

SOLID A

OUTLINE & VEIN IN B.

Outline and Fill Scroll, #8 cut wool. Hooked by Gene Shepherd.

Although we keep insisting that is important to always point your hook at a right angle to the line as it changes direction, this close up underscores the reason why. Technique becomes particularly important as cut size is increased—bigger cuts are more noticeable. Loops from plain wool are also more noticeable. Much more of the loop detail is seen in this rendition than with the tweed wool of the previous project.

The black background really accentuates the center scrolls. While all backgrounds do that to a certain extent, black really turns up the amperage, especially with the "hot" colors of this scroll. Any other choice would dramatically lessen the impact of the piece.

Although not technically a part of this section, the "bead" row around the edge of the rug also plays an important part in the over-all effect. While something was needed to finish off the rug, the piece called out for just the suggestion of a border, not a BORDER. Using the two colors from the scroll, both pieces were used in an alternating fashion as the bead row was hooked down its ditch. This can get a little tricky as the wool hand, under the frame, must control two pieces at the same time. In effect, a loop of color A is brought up in hole #1, then a loop from color B is pulled in hole #2. Hole #3 is skipped. Color A appears in hole #4, etc. While all this is appearing on the top side, the wool hand must go back and forth between the two colored strips of wool on the underneath side of the frame. That hand must keep the pieces flat as they go on the hook and cohabit side-by-side. It takes bit of practice, but the effect is worth the effort.

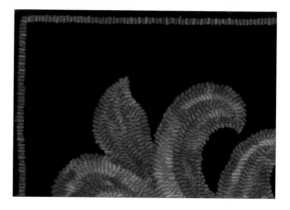

Outline and Fill Double Scroll, 25 $\frac{1}{2}$" x 13", #8-cut wool on monk's cloth. Designed and hooked by Jane Olson and Gene Shepherd. Hooked by Gene Shepherd.

CHAPTER 4

Hooking Prototypes From A–Z

One of the great strengths of *The Rugger's Roundtable* is that it has provided countless rug hookers with directions on how to hook so many different designs over the past 30 years. We've chosen a wide variety of these prototypes, as well as include a few new ones, to provide you with a dictionary of hooking tips for whatever comes your way from A-Z.

Even though Jane's original drawings lean heavily towards fine shading, remember, they can easily be reinterpreted by the wide-cut artist. As evidenced in the last chapter, every design can be done a number of ways. Unless indicated otherwise, all line drawings are by Jane Olson. The initial description is usually a quote or paraphrase from *The Rugger's Roundtable*. Photo captions, however, have been provided by the editor since many of the hooked projects shown are interpretations of Jane's design, not specific illustrations based on her instructions. We think it is important for you to see how different artists adapt her information to their own style or skill level. Hopefully, this will help the reader develop a practical philosophy of hooking so that they can interpret and adapt any set of instructions they might encounter.

Using the work of dozens of Jane's friends and students, these hooked illustrations represent every style, cut, and level of expertise. Feel free to use them any way that helps you express yourself through the medium of hooked rugs.

Fine Shaded Trumpet Illustration. Traditional rug hooking directions usually lean towards a fine shaded orientation. These instructions clearly show the direction one should hook, as well as give clues to where light and dark wool should be used.

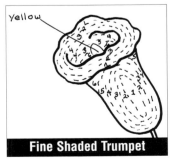

Fine Shaded Trumpet

Primitive Trumpet Illustration. Rug hookers who prefer more "primitive" designs should learn to look at such directions, then run them through their wide cut processor, producing an image that looks like this.

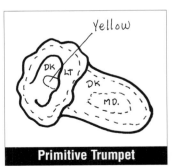

Primitive Trumpet

■ Apple—Since apples can often contain several colors, a plain red or yellow swatch doesn't allow for the variation needed to achieve realism. For that reason, you might like to try "fingering" your strips (described in Chapter 2) of different colors. It is not an easy technique because of the constant cutting. However, it allows you to achieve both gradation and other color highlights. To do this, begin at the bottom of the apple with a dark shade. End the rows of that shade at irregular lengths. As you continue with the next shade, start the rows in between those of the first shade and continue. Again, end at irregular intervals. Finger in spots of additional color or highlights where needed. This takes a little more time than the normal blending of shades, but it gives a definite three-dimensional look to your apple. You will notice at the top of the apple, there are only two or three loops for the shades.

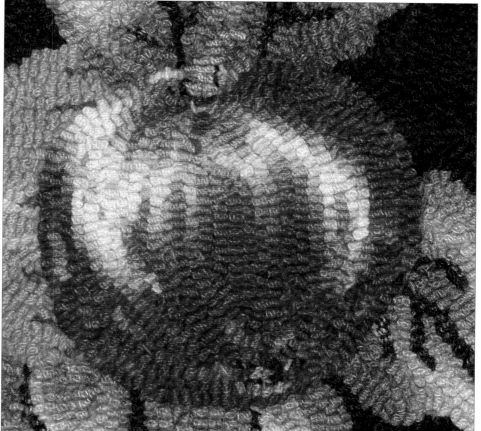

Detail **Dip-Dye Apple,** #4-cut wool. Hooked by Norma Flodman. Gradation and additional color spots can also be achieved with a dip-dye, making for easier hooking. To get that natural "blush," spot dye over your apple using colored wool and then hook your strips in the order you cut them.

■ Apple Blossom and Dogwood—These two flowers are so similar that they are being listed together. However, they do have a few very significant differences. Apple blossoms are usually white to a very light green, with each blossom having five petals. The backside, or turnover, of the petal is a very light pink. The center is yellow and green. Dogwood blossoms come in a white variety, as well as delicate pink. They also have yellow and green centers. While their overall shape and size is very similar to the apple blossom, the turnover indentation is much more pronounced and a darker color. Dogwoods only have four petals. (*I'll Be With You in Apple Blossom Time* is the single most often requested duet of Jane Olson and her sister, Norma Flodman. Actually, they will most probably sing it with out a request.)

Apple Blossom, #3-cut wool swatches. Hooked by Jane Olson.

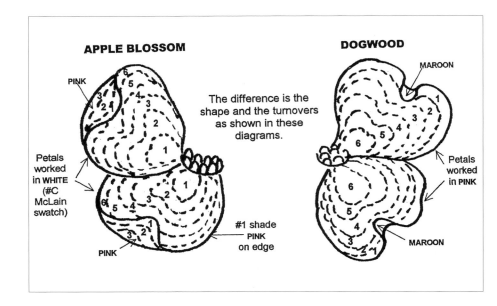

APPLE BLOSSOM

DOGWOOD

The difference is the shape and the turnovers as shown in these diagrams.

PINK

Petals worked in WHITE (#C McLain swatch)

PINK

#1 shade PINK on edge

MAROON

Petals worked in PINK

MAROON

Dogwood Blossoms, #4-cut wool. Hooked by Carla Fortney. For the petals, the artist used various pastel dip-dyes interspersed against white wool in striped fashion. Three or four cycles with the same dip-dye and white against several repetitions on another dip-dye combination give the petal depth. A variety of greens were also dip-dyed for the leaves and hooked in similar stripes.

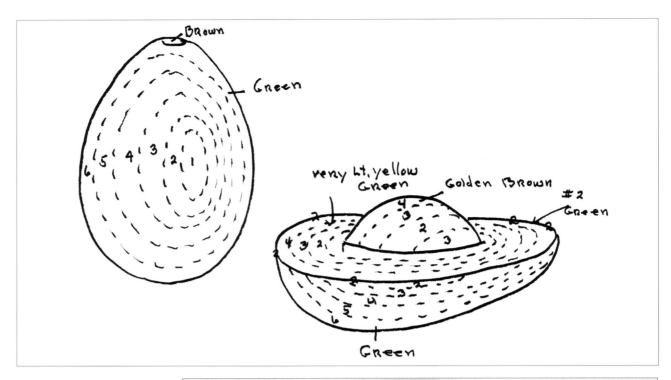

■ Avocado—Avocados are important to Jane, if for no other reason than she eats one every day! That regime, coupled with the fact that she eats virtually no refined sugars, may provide the secret to this octogenarian's stamina and overall good health.

Avocados, #4-cut wool. Hooked by Jane Olson. This is a straight forward fine shaded version. #1 is for the lightest wool and #6 is for the darkest. You will need to use a yellow-green for the center and dark green for the outside. A medium golden brown is appropriate for the pit. Remember to hook in the natural contour of the avocado so that it looks realistic.

■ Backgrounds—Backgrounds can be hooked in several ways. When choosing one, pick something that accentuates rather than competes with your major motifs. Whatever you choose, continue using that same technique throughout the applicable sections of the rug so it will lay flat. This also helps to unify the overall appearance of the piece.

■ Curlicue Starburst—If you have a large section of background at the very center of your rug, use a fabric marker and make a starburst of curlicues emanating from the center. Hook these curlicues, right on the line. Then, go back and just fill in to the point where you reach your design. This sort of technique is particularly useful when the rug has a wreath like design in the middle, with more background to the outside edge. This would require that the lines of the center starburst be continued to the outside border.

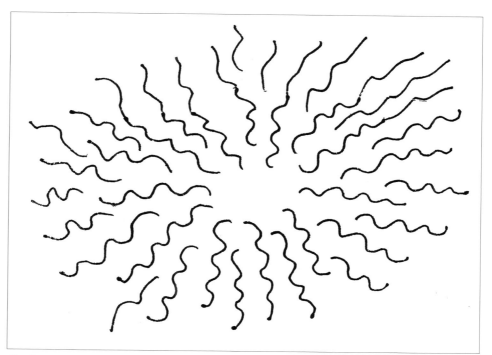
Curlicue starburst

■ Worm Curlicues—After hooking the design, draw worm-like curlicues here and there, all over the background space that needs to be filled. Hook right on those lines and then fill in around them. Some people achieve the same effect by writing the names of their grandchildren or pets in cursive, instead of making the curlicues. This background has a tendency to compete with the major motifs it surrounds, particularly if there is a great deal of color or shade variation in your background wool.

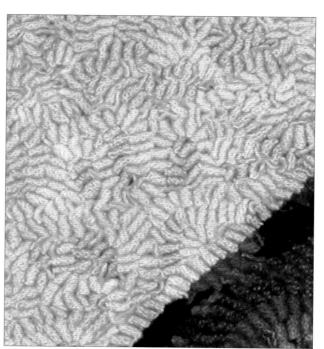
Worm Curlicue Example

Worm curlicue background

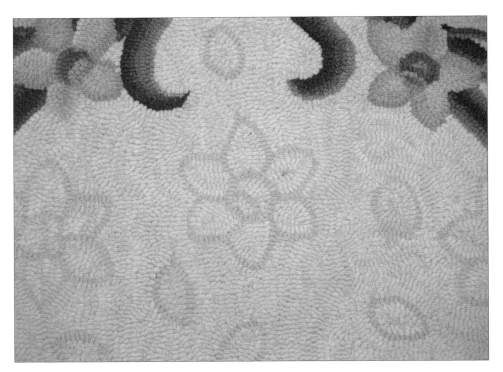

■ Design Repeats—

Instead of making curlicues to start the background, why not repeat some design element used in the rug? In this rug, Jane drew some Jonquils here and there amidst the background. Since the background wool was two very close shades of the same color—one for the center and the other for the outside, she used the "off" colors to outline the flowers and then filled in. It's a nice way to provide interest in a large piece space.

■ Echo Hooking—When a

design is hooked, the usual procedure is to hook two rows of background around that design. As that is being done, also hook two rows on the outside edge of the rug. Continue hooking equal rows from the design out and the edge in.

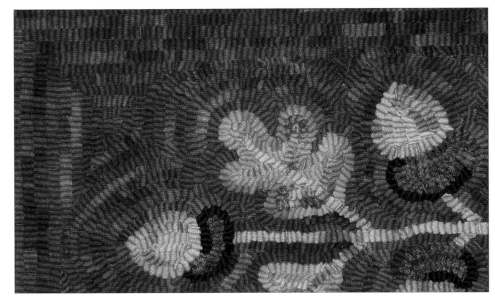

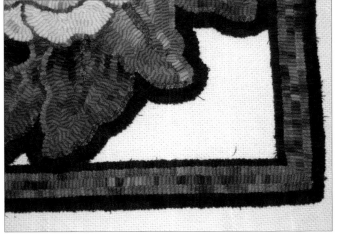

When these rows of hooking meet, an irregular space will be created. Keep hooking concentric rows around this irregular space until it is filled. Continue until all spaces on the rug are filled in. This technique is particularly good when the design is simple. The echo effect makes the design "pop." Since this technique works from the outside in, it's very important that overcrowding not take place.

Gene's Birds, #3, 4, and 5-cut wool. Designed and hooked by Gene Shepherd. Any technique other than straight hooking would have disrupted the peaceful setting of this rug.

■ Straight Hooking—

Plain "straight in the ditch" hooking can be very effective as a background. These parallel rows have a calming effect on the design, as opposed to the movement suggested by curlicue techniques. However, whether the rows are hooked horizontally or vertically, two sides of the rug will end up with rows where the ends stick out as they butt up to the edge and stop. That's not how a rug edge needs to end. The other two rows, since they run the direction of the edge, point their ends away from the edge,

which is the way your finished product should look. To keep this from happening, run at least one row of hooking around all four sides of the piece so those two odd rows have something to butt up against and stop. It could be the color of the background or some other contrasting color that might give just a hint of a picture frame edge. Of course, it could be a much wider picture frame border as well. Even with this, however, you will still have two sides where all of the rows come to the same edge and stop. This would

be a good time to employ the tail end staggering technique covered in Chapter 2 so you don't end up with two long rows of tails.

Franklin Delano Roosevelt's Presidential Flag Rug, 60" x 43", #3, 4, 5, and 6-cut wool on monk's cloth. Recreated for Top Cottage, Hyde Park, New York, and hooked by Gene Shepherd, Anaheim, California, 2004. This is the type of design which benefits from this sort of background. Any non-conformity of rows would ruin the impact of the piece. While it is a bit of extra effort to do, it pays off when the rug is as simple a design as this.

■ **Straight Hooking with turned corners—**

This is straight, in the ditch hooking, where only the four straight sides of the rug are echoed. All corners are strictly turned on the mitered corner line with your method of choice. This really is one of those times when it is best to work from the center out, particularly if it is a big rug with a lot of background.

1. If the rug is 3' x 5', the center horizontal ditch would be in the middle of the rug, or 1½' in from the two long sides. Draw a foot long line down that ditch.

2. Measure in 1½' from the two shorter sides and place a dot on the exact spot. Bring the first ditch line over so that the line stops in the spots you have just measured. You should have a 2' long line on the 1½' center horizontal ditch. It should also stop and start exactly 1½' in from each vertical edge.

3. From these starting and stopping points at each end of the ditch, draw a straight line to each corner. This will set the mitered corner turn line.

4. If the very center is hooked in background, hook the 2' base line right on the line. Start and stop at the point where the mitered lines converge. The second row of hooking will go around this center straight line with corner turns precisely on the mitered lines. Determine the ditch for this new row and make sure it is followed on all four sides of the rectangle. This must be followed in rigid fashion. Whenever a new row starts around the perimeter, all four sides need to be in the same ditch away from the previous row.

5. If the center has no background, then count (not measure) out the number of holes that it takes to get past the center design. If it takes 100 holes, then count out 100 on each side of your 2' line and 100 from the exact hole where the line starts and stops. Extend the lines so that they intersect. If they do not intersect exactly on the diagonal line already drawn, your count was wrong. Go back and recheck to find the right spot. The holes need to be counted because backings stretch while being measured. This uninterrupted rectanglar line should allow uninterrupted hooking until the edge. To fill in back towards the center design, hook straight, broken lines. As these lines butt up to design elements, you may want to stagger the tail ends.

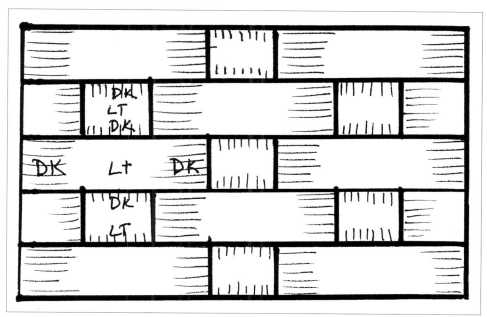

Basket Illustration

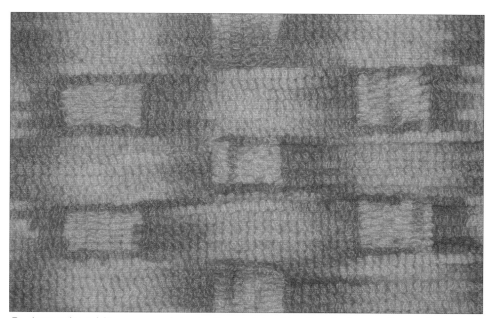

Baskets take a bit more work to do than bricks. Use the darker sections of your wool to outline the longer horizontal strips of the basket material so they show up against the vertical pieces. The leftover light sections can be saved for the vertical sections of the basket. The full 16″ pieces will be used for the horizontal sections.

■ Basket and Bricks—

The easiest way to do a brick or basket pattern is with a dip-dye. Since both rectangular designs have dark on either end with a light center, dip dye each piece of wool so it goes from dark to light, back to dark. If the length of the brick is 4", the dip dyed piece would need to be about 16" long. Jane first dips the whole piece of wool in a very light shade of whatever color she is dyeing to lessen the stark-ness of the white or natu-ral colored wool. Tint the clear water in the dye pot with just a teaspoon of whatever dye mixture you have prepared, remove the wool from the tinted water

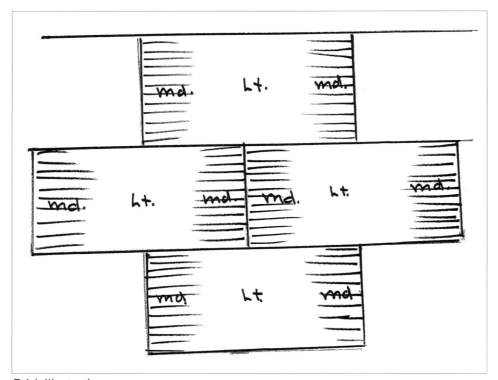

Brick Illustration

and add the rest of the dye mixture to the pot. Fold the 16" long piece of wool in half so that it makes two 8" sections. Holding the wool at the fold, dip just the ends in the dye at the same time. Proceed as you would for a dip-dye, lowering the wool a bit at a time, making sure the lightest section is at the fold. When done, the 16" piece will go dark to light to dark.

When hooking bricks, outline each brick with a contrasting color. It can be something that is either very dark or very light, depending on the type of mortar you wish to portray.

■ Bell—In order for the bell to have some depth, there must be a "shining" lighter section. This section, containing the lightest values, should not be at dead center on the bell. For depth, work the inside area around the clapper with darker wool so that this section seems to be in a bit of a shadow. Proceed towards the bottom of the bell with slightly lightened values.

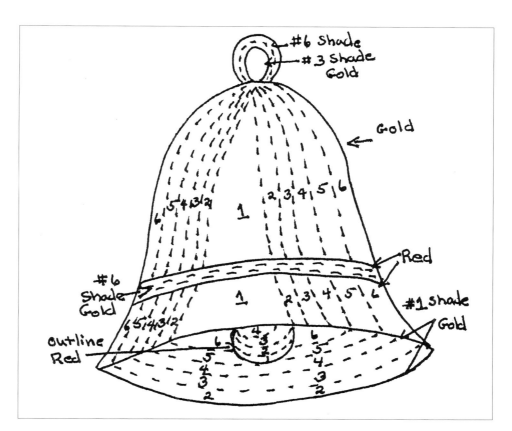

Bell detail, #3-cut wool. Hooked by Jane Olson.

Detail **Blackberry,** #3-cut wool. Hooked by Jane Olson.

Blackberry Illustration

■ **Blackberries**—Save yourself a lot of time and trouble when hooking blackberries by over dyeing a piece of black and white check with a plum colored dye. Do not stir after adding the wool to the dye bath so that it will come out with vivid mottling. Just cutting and hooking will give variation. If more is needed, use a little plain black wool to help define the shape of the berry.

■ **Blueberries**—Blueberries are so small that you don't have a lot of space to worry about. If you want to use swatches there is only room for just the suggestions of four or five values. As with blackberries, you can simplify the process with mottled blue wool, making sure that a light piece ends up where a highlight ought to be. Blueberries always have a

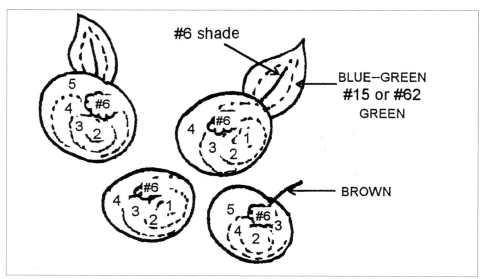

Blueberries Illustration

dark "dimple." Hook a dark section on one side of that dimple and a lighter shade the other to make it stand out. Blueberries also need a highlight somewhere on the fruit. This spot should be varied from berry to berry. It can also be hooked with different values of your lighter shades.

Detail of **Blueberries,** #4-cut wool. Hooked by Norma Flodman.

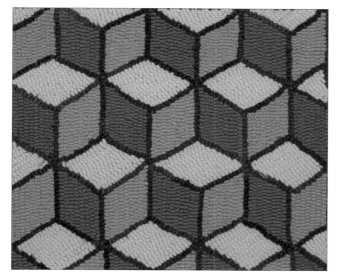

Blocks, #6-cut wool. Hooked by Robin Page.

■ **Blocks**—Striking three-dimensional effects can be achieved with just three shades or values as shown in the diagram. By hooking the sides of the block vertically, they will appear higher. By hooking them horizontal, they appear smaller. It is best to outline them, right on the design line, before filling in so that the shape will be more pronounced. Any time you do a geometric design, work very hard to do each block side or section exactly the same as the others. If you want to be exact, count the number of loops you put in the first line of a section and then repeat that same number of loops in every line of every block.

■ **Buildings**—When working a row of buildings, outline the ones that you want to appear closer to you in a darker color. Those sitting further back can be outlined in a medium color. Next, outline the windows with the darkest shade that you are going to use for that particular building. Fill the inside of the windows with different gray wools. Something as simple as alternating the direction you hook the rows of each building will help define each structure and give them a more distinct appearance.

Buildings, #5-cut scrap wool. Hooked by Sharon Saknit.

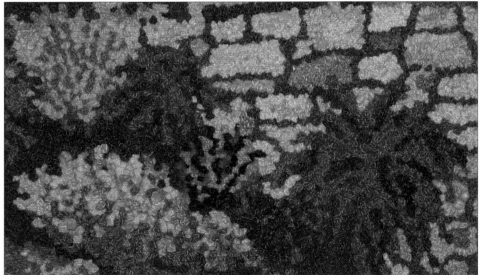

Detail, **The Covered Bridge,** #3 cut-wool. Designed by Paul Detlefsen. Hooked by Jane Olson.

■ **Bushes**—When hooking any bush, it's good to use at least three or four different pieces of wool in the same general family. They can be solid colors, mottled or spot dyed over plain or textured wool. When hooking more than one of the same kinds of bush, make sure that you use different combinations of shades in the different bushes. Some bushes in the same family can be lighter when in the foreground and darker when behind other bushes. This will help make bushes of the same family stand out. If other kinds of bushes are in the same design, then use a completely different combination of wool pieces to make them stand out. Adopt a different hooking direction to represent a different bush type. In this picture, one type of bush has arching branches; another has more vertical branches while the third has a more horizontal look. Each type has its own distinct color scheme.

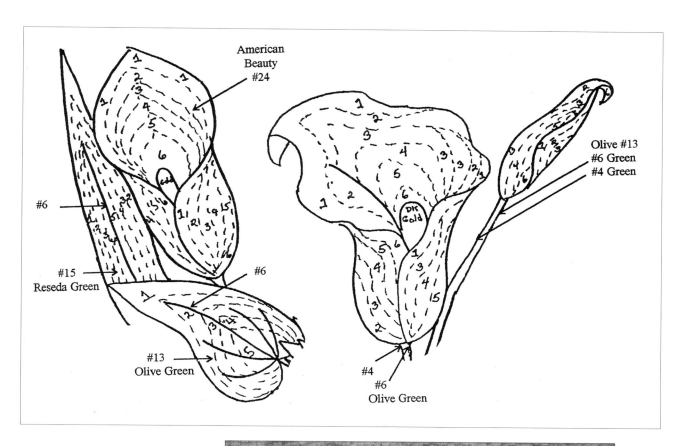

American Beauty #24

Olive #13
#6 Green
#4 Green

#6

#15
Reseda Green

#13
Olive Green

#4
#6
Olive Green

Dk Gold

■ **Calla Lily**—When doing Calla Lilies, start in the center of the throat and work out to the top. Next, work the base of the throat on the right side and end with the base of the throat on the left. These sorts of flowers now come in many different colors. The traditional version would go from green, in the throat, to a pure white on the edge. I also like to hook them going from gold to red.

Detail of **Calla Lilly,** #4- and 5-cut wool with swatch. Hooked by Jane Olson.

■ **Cat's Paws**—Cat's paws, mille fleur, or jewels are different names for the same tried and true rug hooking motif—the round shape of Chapter 2 hooked with a succession of dazzling colors. They can be spaced rigidly or at random locations on your design, in one size or many. They don't even have to be round. Always start in the center of your "paw" with a three-point triangle made up of two loops and a hole with the beginning and ending tail. Then, encircle that triangle with a round row of hooking. Start and stop in the same hole. Do the same thing for each successive row until you have a cat's paw the size you want.

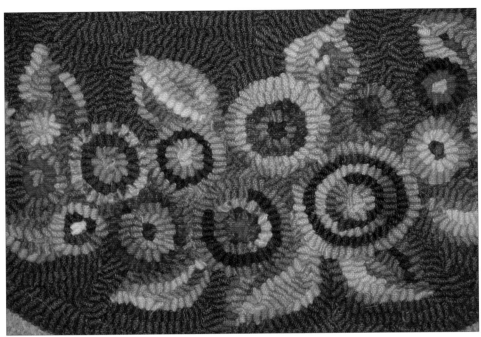

Detail of **Cat's Paws,** #6-cut wool on monk's cloth. Designed and hooked by Gene Shepherd.

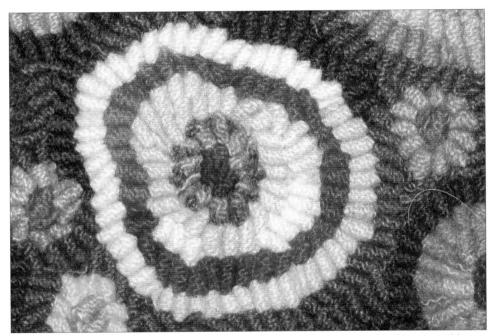

For irregular amoeba shapes, start with a round center as described here and in Chapter 2. Two or three rows out, add a little hooked growth of the last color you used in two or three places. The next hooked row will pick up that irregular shape.

■ **Cardinal**—When doing any animal or bird, hook the eye first. Next, hook the beak. Then, hook black around both eye and beak. When done, you can hook the rest of the head, making sure to hook in the natural directional lines of the body. To do the wing, start at the top and work down. Don't forget that there is a small portion of wing sticking out from the right side. Be sure to fill in this little area as it will add realism to your bird. After doing the wing, give yourself a break and do the easiest part—the breast. You can finish up with the tail feathers. For the male cardinal, a bright red swatch is perfect, whether you do it with a fine cut or something much wider. The female cardinal is a brownish gray bird with reddish highlights. Jane used a golden swatch instead of a brown one because she wanted a brighter finished product.

Cardinals, #3-cut wool. Hooked by Jane Olson.

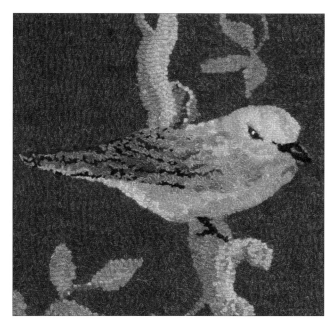

Finch, #3-cut wool. Designed and hooked by Marion Wise. Even though this a totally different bird, the basic hooking directions given for the cardinals still apply, with the exception of the colors to be used. The artist also effectively substituted a variety of scrap wool to get the subtle variations in the wing and breast, instead of using swatches.

Primitive Bird, #6-cut wool. Hooked by Jane Olson. With very little effort, this primitive bird could be turned into a primitive version of Jane's female cardinal. All that is needed is to add a bit of black to the throat and eye, as well as a pointy-head. The female cardinal of the line drawing could also be hooked in this fashion, using a wide cut, with just two colors and a simplified eye. The same could be done with the male, using two shades of red.

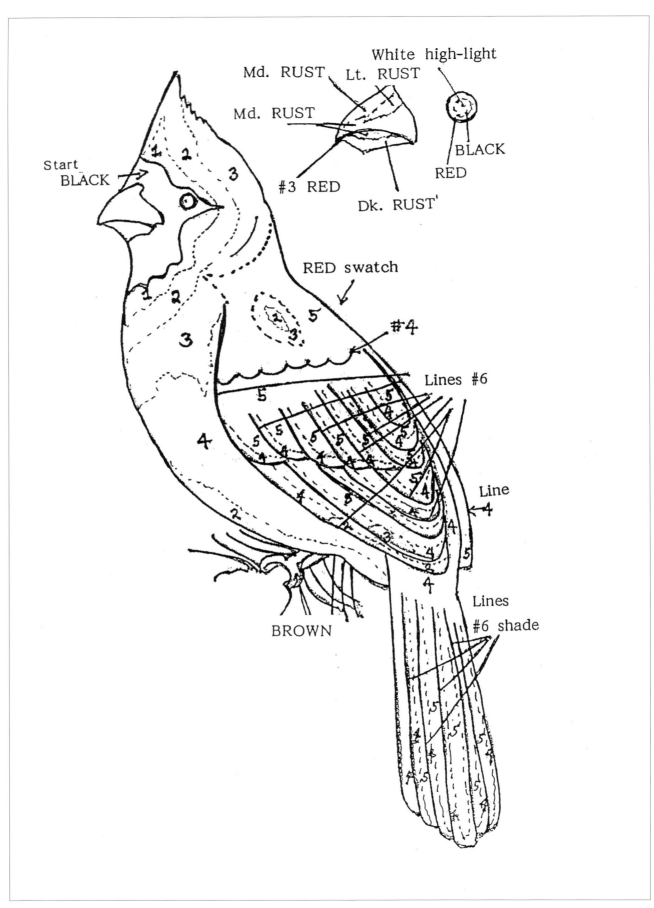

Male Cardinal

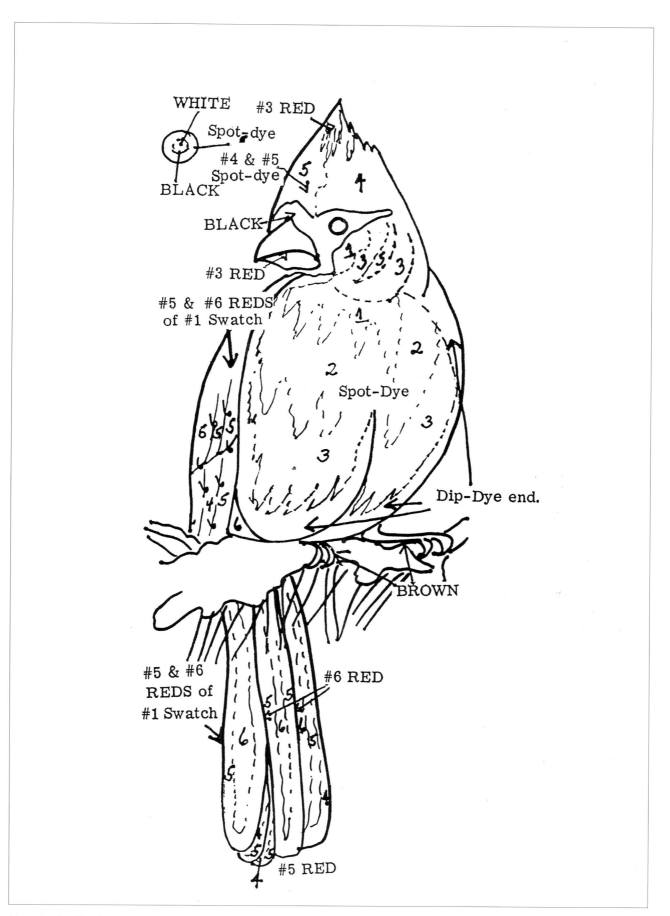

Female Cardinal

■ Cherries—Cherries come in shades of bright red, burgundy, or yellow with a blush of red. Cherries can be improved with two things – a dark indentation line of your darkest color where the stem connects to the fruit, and a highlight of your lightest color on the fruit where it would catch the light. When using a swatch, all six shades do not have to be used in each cherry. Some can be darker and some can be lighter, since that's the way they are found on the tree. Again, fruit highlights are never in the same place on each piece of fruit.

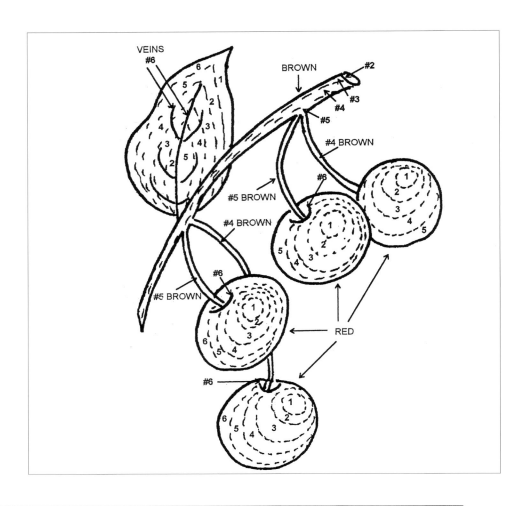

Cherries, #4-cut wool. Hooked by Norma Flodman.

■ Chrysanthemum—

This style of chrysanthemum is not very popular in traditional rug patterns because of the number of turnovers in the petals. However, all the turnover petals are worked the same way. Start with petal #1, the petal that is on top of all the rest, and then work down numerically to the 56th petal. Generally speaking, the turnover sections are done with the three lightest values and the interior part of the petal is worked with the three darker values. The exception to this rule would be the light outline on the interior sections of the dark petals. This is needed so those dark sections will stand out.

Chrysanthemum, #3-cut wool. Hooked by Sharon Saknit.

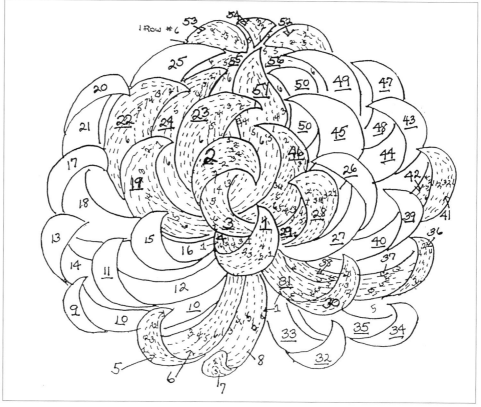

Chrysanthemum Illustration

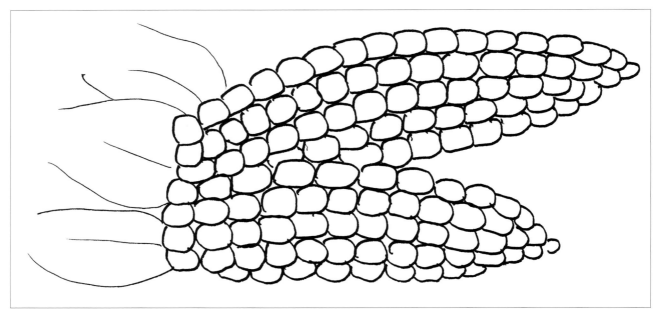

Corn Illustration

■ **Corn**—The individual kernels of this design could be hooked with a fine cut in much the same fashion as the directions for grapes. However, one #8-cut per row does the job much faster.

Corn detail, **Give Thanks Runner,** #8-cut wool. Hooked by Gene Sheherd, 2004.

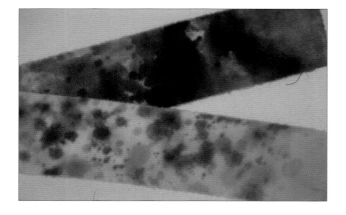

Using different combinations of gold, plum, blue, and magenta dyes, spot dye one piece of wool that leans towards dark and another that leans towards light. When finished, the wool should have recognizable leopard-like spots. Make sure that some of the white wool is not dyed. The choice of a #8-cut, hooked in rows, helps replicate the realistic look of Indian corn. When the design calls for yellow corn, use a spot dye with different medium intensities of the same color. The cornhusks were hooked by with #5-cut wool cut by Jane using a swatch.

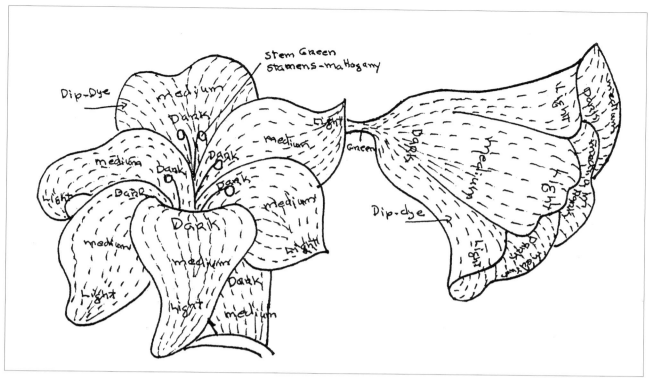

Day Lily Illustration

■ **Day Lily**—I suggest a dip-dye for day lilies. Put the lightest end on the outside of the petals and the darkest on the inside. Do the stamens first with a very dark mahogany color. When working the petals, be sure to do the top petals first. If you need a dividing line between the petals, use the medium section of the dip-dye in both the dark and light areas. If using swatches, the petals do not need dividing lines. When hooking the half-closed flower, work a little of the green from the stem up into the flower.

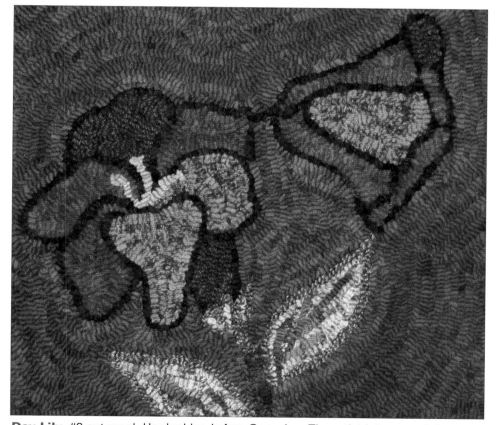

Day Lily, #8-cut wool. Hooked by JoAnn Gonzalez. The artist interpreted the drawing with a wide cut, outline and fill rendition. After hooking on the design lines with very dark textured wool, she filled in with three values of similar wool—two pieces were textured and one piece was mottled. As per Jane's directions, the stamens were done first with a contrasting color.

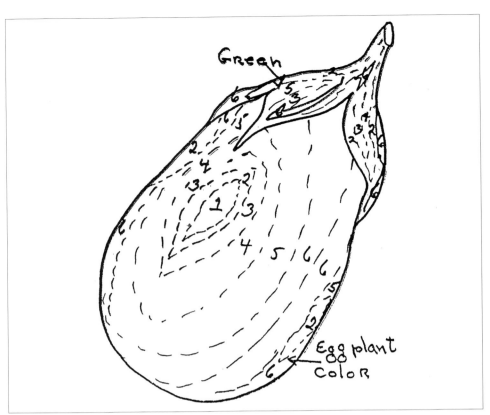

Eggplant Illustration

Eggplant—This is a good eggplant formula for an $^1/_8$ of a yard of wool using Cushing Dyes: $^1/_8$ teaspoon Purple, $^1/_8$ teaspoon Mulberry, $^1/_{16}$ teaspoon Blue, $^1/_{64}$ teaspoon Black. There are lots of dye books that give the instructions for making a 6-value swatch, should you wish to do so. A lazy swatch is easier—just tear the wool into four pieces. Place dye and mordant in the pot and bring to the simmer. Place the wool, one piece at a time, in the dye bath in intervals of 45 seconds to one minute or a little more. Stirring produces an even color. Mottling will result if you do not stir. (See Pumpkin) When hooking, always follow the contour of the design as suggested by the broken lines. It will give the eggplant dimension.

Egg Plant, #8-cut scrap wool. Hooked by Sharon Saknit. Dark solids, medium to light spot dyes, and plaids came out of the artist's scrap bag for this interesting rendition.

■ Fern Leaves—These leaves can be hooked with swatches, dip-dyes, mottled and spot-dyed check or tweed. Remember to start with the veins and stem. When using a swatch, don't feel compelled to use all or even the same combination of the values in every leaf. For a primitive version, do the two sides of the leaf in different colors or half the leaves in a light shade with the other half in a dark shade.

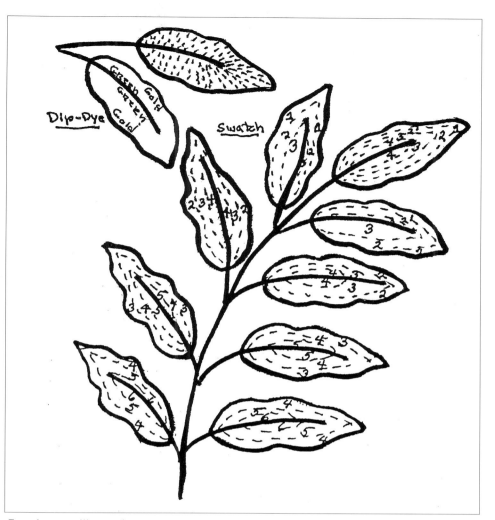

Fern Leaves Illustration

Fern Leaves, #4-cut wool. Hooked by Jane Olson.

■ **Flower Pot**—Plain rust is a very dull color. To brighten it up, use equal parts of Terra Cotta and Rust when dyeing. To give definition, hook a row of Dark Brown along both the top and bottom of the forward top rim. This will distinguish the top from the base of the pot, as well as give depth and perspective. The visible top rim at the back of the pot should be hooked in your darkest value of Terra Cotta.

Detail, **Flower Pot,** #8-cut wool. Hooked by Jane Olson.

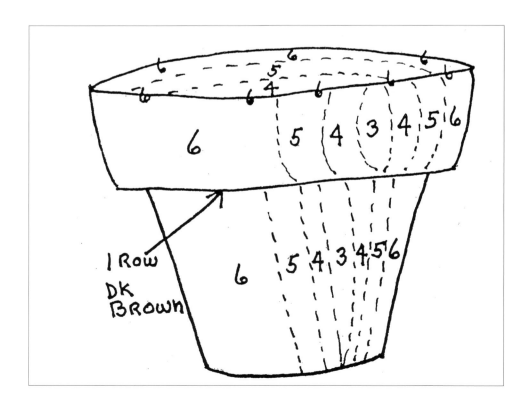

■ **Geometrics**—While the repetitive nature of a geometric design does simplify as well as dictate the artist's work, geometrics are anything but simple. If you want a project to help you hone your hooking skills, do a geometric. Having to repeat and replicate the same design over and over in the same piece is quite a challenge since any variation tends to stick out. Geometrics help beginners acquire hooking skills and challenge experienced hookers to expand their hooking skills.

Triangle detail from **Miss Weigle,** #6-cut wool. Designed and hooked by Gene Shepherd.

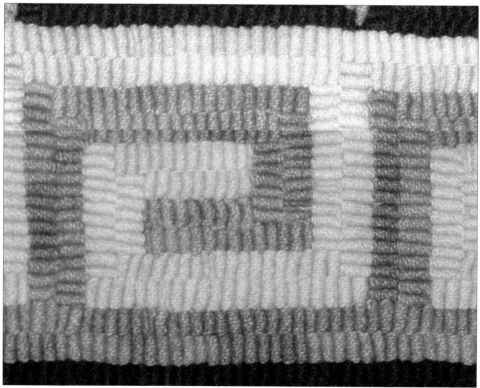

Everything in this rug is hooked with a #6 cut. However, since no combinations of #6 filled the Greek Key perfectly, a switch was made to two rows of #8, which provided the perfect fit.

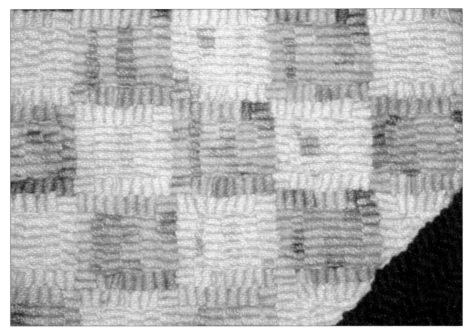

Checkerboard detail from **Miss Weigle**. Designed and hooked by Gene Shepherd. In the checkerboard, take special care to begin each new square by hooking the perimeter sides in the same row over from the ditch. If it is one row over from the design line or two rows over, then make sure to do it the same way for every single square in the checkerboard. Turn all of the corners in exactly the same way. When it comes time to fill, fill them all exactly the same way. When a third color is used to outline, hook that color right on the line. Hook all the grid lines first and then fill in all the squares exactly the same way.

Here are some tips to follow when doing Geometrics:

1. Make sure the pattern is drawn straight. That means north/south and east/west lines will not only be in a ditch, but that (in the case of a checkerboard for example) all the lines of a design that continue the length or width of the piece will be in the same ditch. You cannot draw a geometric by just tracing designs on a light box. You must make exact measurements. Once the proper ditch line is found, it must be followed the length or width of the piece. When buying a geometric pattern, pay very close attention to the exactness of the producer. If you see design lines wandering off and on their ditch, take it as a warning signal not to buy.

2. Experiment with cut size before you begin. The normal practice when doing a project is to pick a cut size and use it throughout. Since geometrics tend to be based on rigid repetitive grids, whatever is experienced for one grid should be the same for another. If one grid fills in perfectly with a certain number of strips, the others should too. If one grid ends with an odd space too small for the cut size being used, all the other grids should too. If your grid has an odd space to fill, experiment. A different cut size might perfectly fill the grid with no odd pieces. If no single per-

fect cut size can be found, then determine the cut of the odd piece and use a combination of the two.

3. Don't force fat pieces into skinny spaces. Even though experienced hookers find themselves presented with left over spaces that are too little for the strip they are using, so many just force a big strip in anyway and go on. In a swirling background, that might not make such a difference now and then. However, such technique, when hooking geometrics, will distort the shape and affect the appearance of your work. When confronted by odd space or row, stop and hand cut something that will fit just right. It will help achieve that rigid shape you are trying to replicate.

4. Experiment with technique. When starting a new grid, hook it a couple of ways to see if one approach works better than another. For example, turning a corner without cutting produces one effect with a #5 and another effect with a #10. (See squares in chapter 2) A little experimentation with cut size and row direction before hooking a new section can pay off big dividends.

5. Pay attention to what you do and then repeat it faithfully. Once settling on a way to hook a motif in a geometric, rigidly follow that formula for each successive repeat.

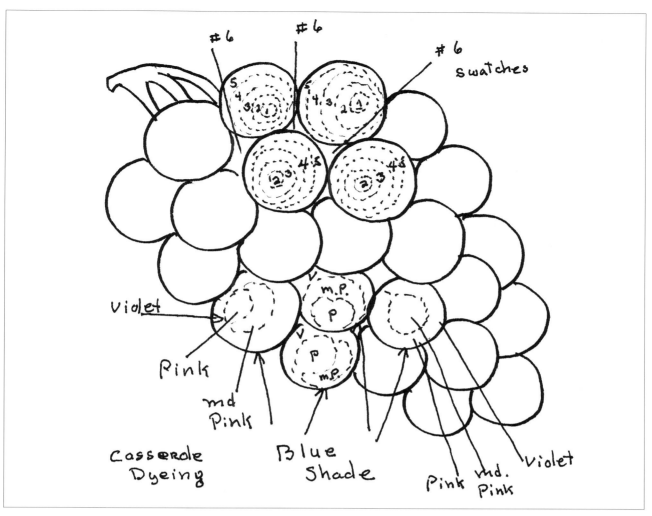

■ **Grapes**—Effective grapes can be made in a variety of ways. The most precise way is to use a swatch in a narrow cut. With such a small design, all the values may not fit in each grape. Grapes aren't exactly the same color anyway, so use whatever combinations of values that look right to you. Some grapes can be darker and others lighter.

Grapes, #3-cut wool swatch. Hooked by Norma Piper.

Detail, **Spot Dye Grapes,** #4-cut wool. Hooked by Jane Olson.

Spot dyes also work well for grapes. Do not hook whole strips of wool for every grape. It is important to use the darkest strips where definition is needed and the lighter pieces for accent. Dark, solid companion wool will provide extra definition between grapes. By spooning two or more colors over the wool, a "natural" unplanned gradation will result.

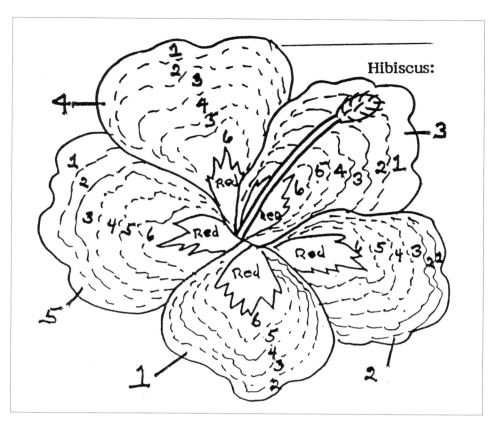

■ Hibiscus—This is a very easy flower to hook. The common variety is white with very deep red spots at the base of the petals. The spike coming out of the center is also dark red. The pollen tip of the spike is gold. When hooking this flower, work the spike first. Hook the petals in the sequence numbered in the diagram. Other colors of hibiscus are pink, rose, yellow, purple, red, blue.

Hibiscus, #3-cut wool. Hooked by Kristi Boren.

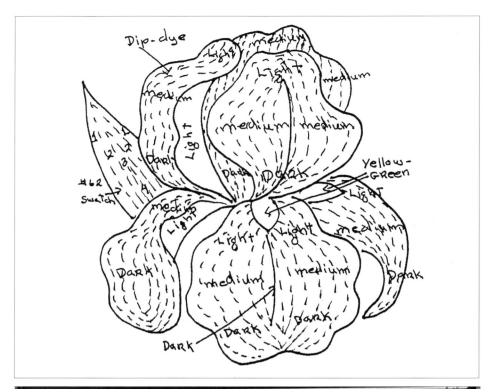

■ **Iris**—This rendition was simplified for a "stained glass" version. Dip-dyes are perfect for an iris. Hook the yellow, yellow/green beard first. Hook the dip-dye from the center out. By alternating the petals light to dark and then dark to light as marked, it will make all the petals stand out. The little "vein" in the petal can be a thin sliver of the dip-dye hooked in reversed color direction to whatever was used in the petal.

Iris, #3-cut dip-dyed wool. Hooked by Jane Olson.

Jonquil—When hooking any flower where all of the petals are the same color, vary the way the 6 values are used in each petal. For example, start with the #1 on the edge of one petal and use all values until ending with #6 on the other side of that same petal. Another petal could have the darkest shade in the center, working out to the lightest shades on each edge. Still another petal could be just the reverse, with light in the center and dark on both edges. Variation will only make the different petals look more natural. The jonquil is distinguished from the daffodil by the shape and smaller size of its center. When hooking the center of a jonquil, think of it as a separate little cup-like flower sitting on top of the other petals. These are usually a different color than the bigger petals.

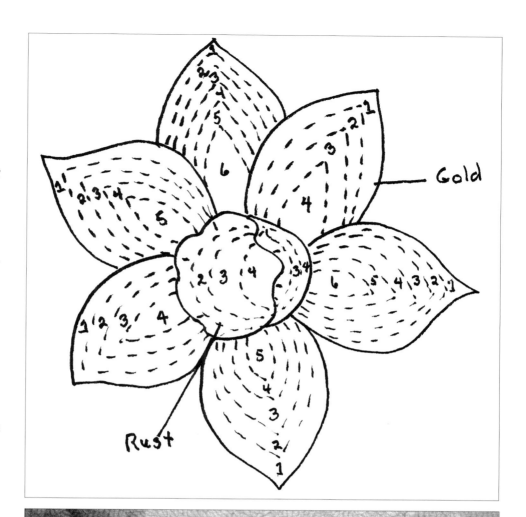

Jonquil, #5-cut wool. Hooked by Jane Olson.

Detail, **Give Thanks Runner.** Hooked by Gene Shepherd, 2005.

The guide rows of background are clearly visible in this photo. Since there is a second line of lettering above the first row—those letters also have two base rows up and two down—there are actually four rows of horizontal hooking, which exist between the two rows of lettering. This provides not only the ruled lines on which to hook the letters to hook, but the proper spacing that is needed between lines. Repeat the same spacing should you need more rows of lettering.

■ **Lettering**—If the piece calls for a cursive, free form sort of lettering, just hook the letters and then hook background on each side. Usually, after doing that, the original lettering needs to be removed and re-hooked. The letters are sharper the second time when hooked "into" the background. If you need to put in a few extra loops on this second pass, do so as it will make the letters nice and full.

If the lettering is printed on a straight line, then these suggestions will help you achieve that regimented look.

1. Hook two rows of background to define the bottom line where the letters will sit and two rows to define the top line towards which the letters will rest. This creates wool lined "paper" on which to hook

the letters.

2. Determine the midpoint on the lettered line. Using THANKS on the bottom row of lettering as the example, the middle is actually the space between the A and the N. Hook two vertical rows of background at the exact center point of where the word is to be. THANKS will be hooked from the center space out.

3. Determine the width of the letters. The letters in these photos are fairly big —about 16 holes across. From the two vertical rows, count over 16 holes on either side and hook two more vertical space rows. This will create a letter box each for A and N. Keep moving out 16 holes, marked by two vertical

rows of background, until enough letter boxes have been created for THANKS. Should a line contain more than one word, work out from the center point of that entire line. Space between words with four or five vertical rows instead of the usual two. Compensate for skinny letters. "I" wouldn't need the full 16 holes, etc.

4. Hook the letters inside the boxes. Make sure the letters rest on the bottom line and reach to both the tops and sides of the box. Once hooked they can be filled in with background.

5. Be repetitive in approach. Always "round" the corners in exactly the same way. If the letter has a mid-section, always try and use the same horizon-

tal ditch for that mid-section in every letterbox where it is needed. This takes counting, but is worth the effort.

6. To make both upper and lower case letters, do everything the way that has been described with one addition. Add a single, middle horizontal line that will be the top base line for the lower case letters. The end result will be like the ruled paper first graders use when they write. If the letter needs to go above, or in the case of G, below the line, then hook to the base line, cut a gate through it and continue. Count holes as it is important to have letters like T, F and I all end at the same ditch line. After a box or two, this process becomes second nature and takes out all the guesswork.

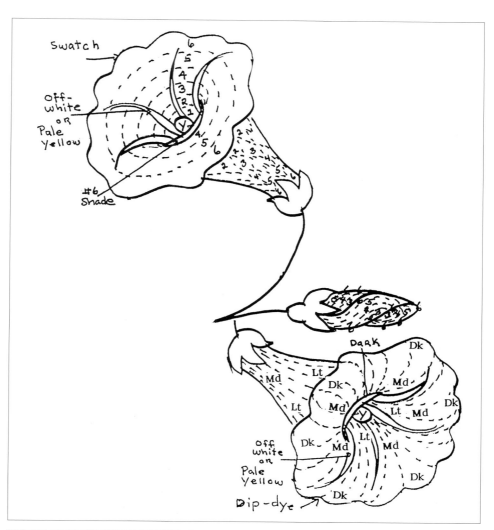

■ **Morning Glory**—I like a blue dip-dye, tipped at the lightest end with a bit of wild rose, for morning glories. Start down in the throat of the flower and hook out to the lightest section of wool. Hook out to a dark edge. Stripes in the flowers can be worked with a pure white or white with a tint of yellow. There are all sorts of variations with blues and purples for this flower. If using swatches, start in the center of the throat with the lightest shade. Hook around the throat with that shade. Work in the other shades, going from light to dark. Continue to hook around the flower throat until the edge. Hook the rest of the flower in the direction drawn.

Morning Glory, #9-cut wool. Hooked by Jane Olson.

Mountains—Mountains were made for spot dyes. I like to use combinations of turquoise blue, olive green, dark gray and silver gray. Greens, browns, and even purple are other possible color families. The mountains or hills in the foreground will use the darkest colors. Each successive range will lessen in color intensity as it recedes. The furthest mountains should be the lightest—the closest the darkest. Follow the contour of the mountains when hooking.

Mountains, #6-cut wool. Hooked by Florence Aguinaldo.

■ Peach—Start with the lightest shade of the dip-dye at the top of the fullest part of the peach. Hook back to the left using lighter wool to create a large ripe section with just a bit of dark at the outside edge. On the right side of the crease, hook the darkest shade of the dip-dye. From that dark section, gradually work to the right, ending with lighter wool at the edge. The bottom tip is always very dark. When using dip-dyes, don't be afraid to use only a section of the wool and then cut. If light wool is needed in a spot, cut as darker wool starts to show up on the strip. Add in another piece of light and continue. Save left over cut sections, as they will probably be needed somewhere else. You are in control of the wool, so make it work for you.

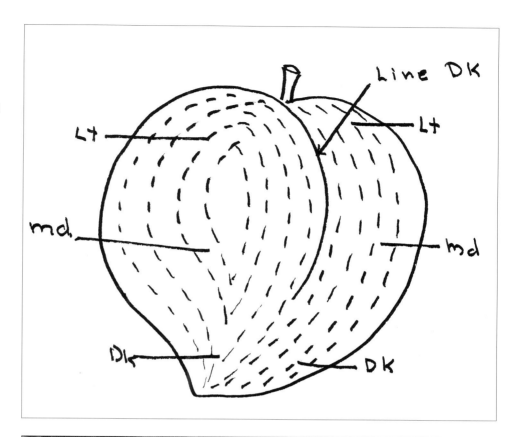

Peach, #4-cut dip-dyed wool. Hooked by Norma Flodman.

Pear—To make a pear, I like to spot dye over a regular swatch. I first soak a yellow or bronze gold swatch in hot water and vinegar and then use a spoon to sprinkle the ends with a little diluted scarlet dye. I use the spoon again to dribble little bits of diluted ocean green over the entire swatch. You can then wrap it in foil and place it in a 350-degree oven for 30 minutes. I like to start with the scarlet ends at the bottom and work up.

Pear, #4-cut wool. Hooked by Norma Flodman.

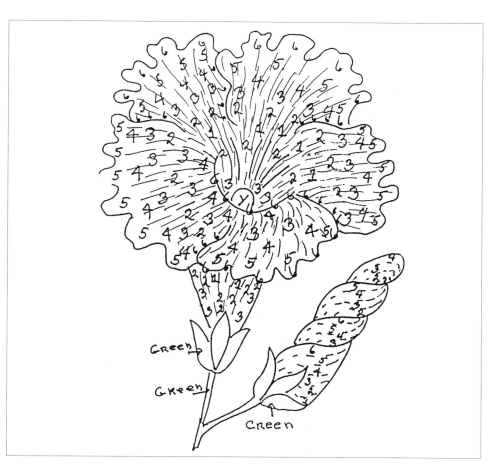

Petunia—Petunias are great flowers to hook. They have no truly divided petals, only deep slits in the flower, which only give the impression of separate petals. The pistil is hooked first with yellow or gold. Hook the line under the pistil next using a dark shade. The diagram is for those who want to "finger" the shades. It takes some work to do this but the end result is worth the effort. For those who do not want to go to such effort, you might consider an outline and fill version. A dark outline wool for the edges and deep slits of the flower will certainly define the shape. As drawn, I have suggested a medium value throat, going to the lightest shades of color at the middle of the petal, then reverse back to the darkest colors at the edge. Two pieces of the same dip-dye would work for this. Have the lighter ends meet in the middle of the petal. One will hook into the throat while the other would hook to the edge.

Petunia, #3-cut wool. Hooked by Susan Andreson.

■ Pine Branch with Snow—Use white and a very light shade of gray to do the snow. The gray should be at the bottom edge of the snow and as definition for ridges. At the end of the branch, work in a little brown. A variety of blue-green wool pieces should be used for the pine needles. The lightest colors of this green would go for the needles "on top" of the others. Darker shades should be used for the needles "under" the others. Hook the needles in straight lines. Hook a few needles into the patches of snow on the branches.

#17 Swatch

WHITE

LT. GREY

WHITE

LT. GREY

#17 Swatch
(BLUE-GREEN)

BROWN

Detail, **Cardinals,** #3-cut wool swatch. Hooked by Jane Olson.

■ Pineapple—When doing a pineapple, do the leaves before the fruit itself. Work the top leaves first. These are very blue-green in color. Start at the bottom with the fruit. Do not get discouraged with the first row of bracts. This is one fruit that has to be completed before you can pass judgment on it. Each bract has to be treated individually. When the fruit is completed you can always change a few things here and there.

Hooked by Anna Boyer; **Pineapple** detail, #7- and 10-cut wool, ultra suede, beads, buttons and organdy ribbon. The artist used a contrast of plain and textured materials to do this mixed media rendition. While #7 was used for the pineapple, the ultrasuede background needed to be done with a #10. Intermittent hooking of organdy ribbon, as well as hand sewn beads and buttons add a nice sparkle to the piece. Leaf shaped pieces were "prodded" in for the top knot.

■ Plaid—It takes a lot of work to hook a plaid design. To draw the design on your backing, carefully count the holes so that the lines are in the same ditches. Hook every section exactly alike—starting and stopping in the same places and putting in the same number of loops, etc. On a design like this, hook the lines first and then fill in. Cuts #3-5 are the best for plaids, with #5 being my preference. Do not crowd as the lines will become distorted.

Plaid, #5-cut wool. Hooked by Jane Olson.

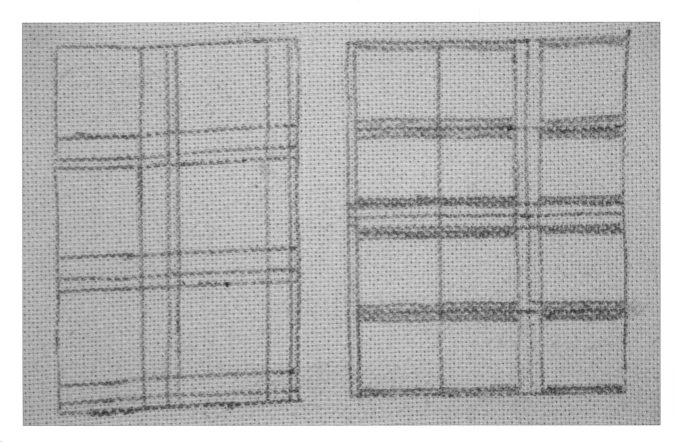

Plum, #4-cut dip dyed wool. Hooked by Norma Flodman.

■ **Plum**—Plums are delicious to eat, colorful to look at, and easy to hook. Whether using swatches or scraps, hook in the direction of the fruit's contour. They are very similar to a peach, and can be hooked in much the same way. I like to dip-dye plum over blue to get a very interesting color.

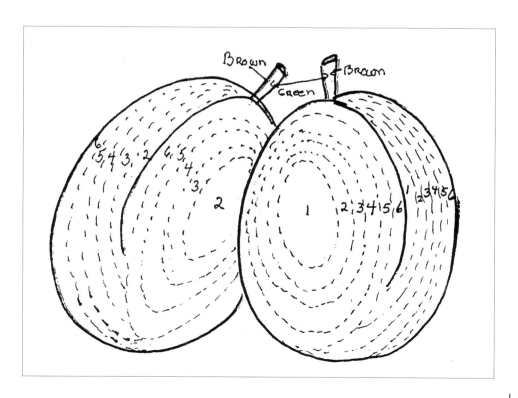

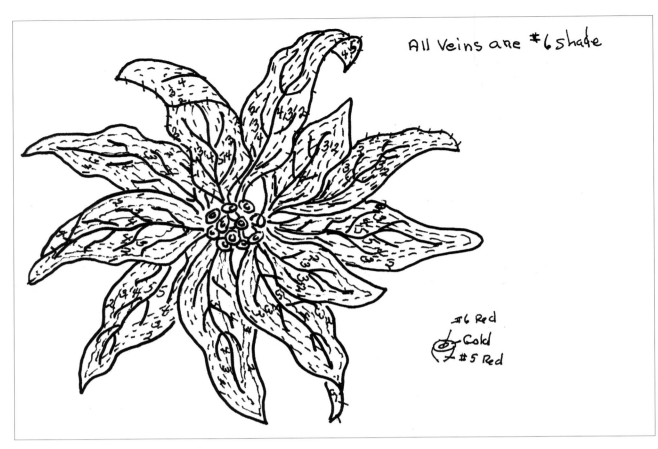

All veins are #6 shade

#6 Red
Gold
#5 Red

■ **Poinsettia**—You only see red and green when looking at a poinsettia,. The petals and leaves are shaded and you can hook them that way to good effect. However, each petal could also be hooked with a different color of red or outlined and filled. With this design, hook the petals on "top" first. That would be in the A, B, C order that is given. The center pods are gold rimmed in red. To make them stand out, outline them in green. While the petals do have many veins, you can eliminate them to make it easier to hook.

Poinsettia, #3-cut wool. Hooked by Susan Naples.

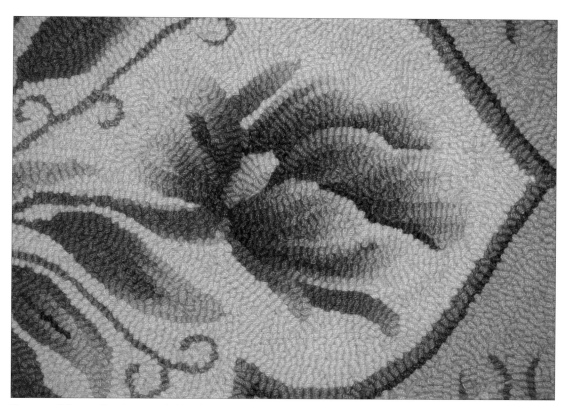

Poppy, #4-cut dip dye wool. Hooked by Jane Olson. In this subdued dip dyed version, Jane started at the top of the petal with the lightest shade, hooking to the darkest at the base.

■ **Poppy**—I like to work poppies with swatches. They are worked with the lightest shade on the out- side of the petals. The color that is recommended is very rich red. When dye- ing, if I can't get it dark enough, I add a little more Turkey Red. The bud is hooked with a green swatch. Hook red where the little petal is showing at the end of the bud. The dots on the green area represent the spiny threads that are on the bud.

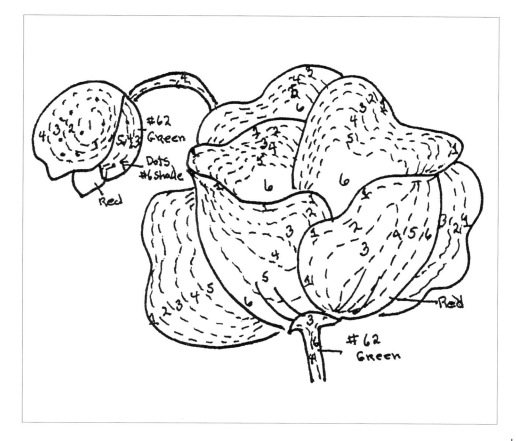

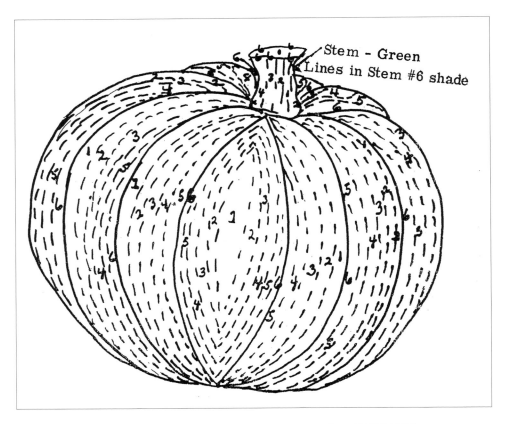

Stem - Green
Lines in Stem #6 shade

■ **Pumpkins**—When working a pumpkin, the ridges must stand out and provide a three-dimensional appearance. This can be accomplished with shading as noted. If you choose a simple scrap method with two or three values, make sure that contrasting colors butt up against each other at the ridges.

Pumpkin, #4-cut wool with a 4-value lazy swatch. Hooked by Jane Olson. (See Egg-plant for lazy swatch directions.) This method is not an exact science, so feel free to add extra pieces or vary the times they are added. If the pieces look the way you want and there is still dye to be absorbed, remove the pieces. Place them in a pan of simmering clear water and mordant until the dye has time to set.

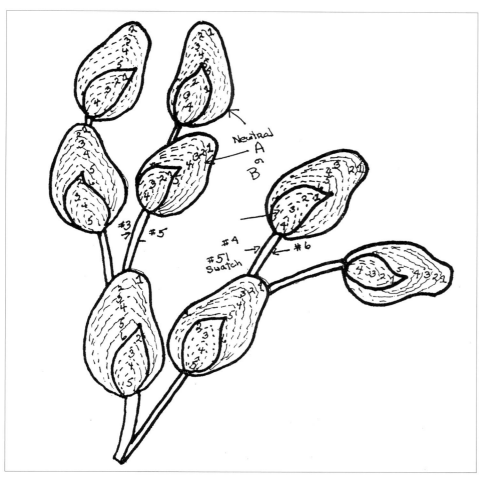

■ Pussy Willow—A harbinger of spring along with the robin, they always add to a bouquet of flowers in a vase or a rug pattern. Use a neutral swatch if you want to shade. Don't try to hook all six values in each one as they are so small. Use the first four or five shades in the top pussy willows and the darker shades for the lower ones. The little caps are so small that they can be hooked solid. Three or four related neutrals could also be used by hooking each little puss in a solid color with a larger cut.

Pussy Willow, #3- and #4-cut wool. Hooked by Marguerite Ryan.

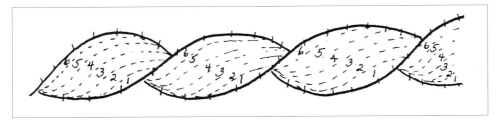

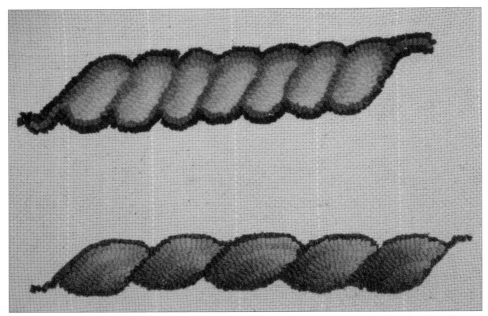

Rope, hooked with #4-cut wool with four-values gold and purple dip dye by Jane Olson.

Shadows detail, **The Covered Bridge** by Paul Detlefsen. Hooked by Jane Olson with a #3-cut wool.

■ **Rope**—Rope is easily hooked with a six-value swatch, for narrow cuts, or three to four values for wider cuts. Repeat order of dark to light as noted in the diagram. Make sure to maintain the arching rope segment shape so as to give a three dimensional appearance. In these two examples, the rope section is shaded side-to-side with the swatch, and end-to-end with the dip-dye.

A "primitive" approach would be to outline all segments with either a light or dark color, filling in with the contrasting shade. Alternating segments in solid light and solid dark would be another option.

■ **Shadows**—Effective shadows are achieved through both color choice and placement. Generally speaking, colors in the shadows go both darker and duller. These colors usually come in to the design along a rigid line, like that dictated by the over hang of this roof. Notice that the bridge colors in the light are vibrant. The section in the shadow is more than just a darker variation; it actually changes to a different related hue.

Shadow detail, **Fog,** #3-cut wool. Designed and hooked by Gene Shepherd. In this design, the entire porch interior is in the shadows, with some parts being more shadowed than the rest, necessitating just two different values of darker wool. The off set porch post shadows and darker sloping roofline against the back wall suggest the impact of the street lap which shines at the right of the house.

Detail, **The Ship,** #3-cut dip dyed wool cut horizontally. Hooked by Jane Olson.

■ **Sky for sunset or sunrise**—The easiest way to hook a sky like this is with a traditional dip-dye. However, it is cut and hooked in a completely different way than usual. While it is dyed vertically, pink to very light blue to medium blue, it is not cut that way. For this application, it is cut and hooked in horizontal rows. The dyed pieces are approximately the length of the sky. The multiple of four needed for hooking would be based on the width. If dyeing a sky that is 10" high and 20" wide, you will need a piece or pieces of wool that were all 10" high and totaled 80" wide. These pieces can be accordion folded and dip-dyed all at once. Be sure to "fluff" the wool as is held in the dye bath so that it will enter the folds of the wool. When finished, the wool should have 80 total inches of a color gradation that is 10" deep. When time to cut, turn the wool on its side, starting at either the top medium blue section or the bottom pink section, and cut one pass through each piece of wool—all 80". These need to be hooked in the order that you cut them. Piece #1, all 80" of it, should be the first one hooked all the way across the horizon. It should then be followed by piece #2 and then #3, etc. Once the first pass of cutting has been hooked in its appropriate rows, go back and make a second cutting through all the wool. Keep track of the rows so you can hook them in their appropriate order. The natural gradation of your dip-dye must be preserved if you want to avoid a striped sky.

Avoid one thing with this method. Since the horizontal rows are all hooked with pieces the same length, the "tails" will all line up in a row unless they are staggered. Start the first piece on each new horizontal row at a different place on the first wool strip. This will stagger the places on the horizontal row where the tails appear.

■ **Snow**—People often ask me: "What color should I use to hook snow?" I don't know what color snow is where you come from, but in California, it's always white! When we add colors to snow, it's because we need to give some definition to the natural and man made ridges that eventually appear in the snow. I usually do this with a very light silver gray swatch. However snow shadows can be hooked in with blue-grays, blues or even purples and pinks, if the snow is being viewed at sunrise or sunset. If stark white is too bright for your particular piece, dip the pure white wool in water lightly tinted with a tiny bit of the color you intend to use for the shadows. Put the white wool in and take it right out. It is important to hook snow in parallel lines. They do not have to be straight, just parallel. Even a subtle change of direction, when coupled with some shadow colors, will underscore "ridge" movement. (See **Pine Branch**.)

■ **Strawberry**—The flowers of the strawberry are almost pure white. When trying to shade them, use only the 4 lightest values. Most berries have a whitish highlight where the sun does not touch them, or they rest against another berry. However, pure white wool would be too stark a contrast. For those highlight spots, dye a piece of white wool with just the slightest bit of Egyptian Red or Bronze Green. It will take off the stark "edge" of white and still produce a highlight that looks appropriate. When hooking the berries, be sure to hook the little sepals on the top first, using a couple different shades of green.

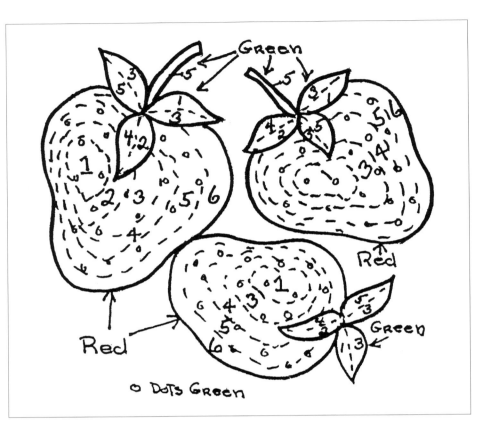

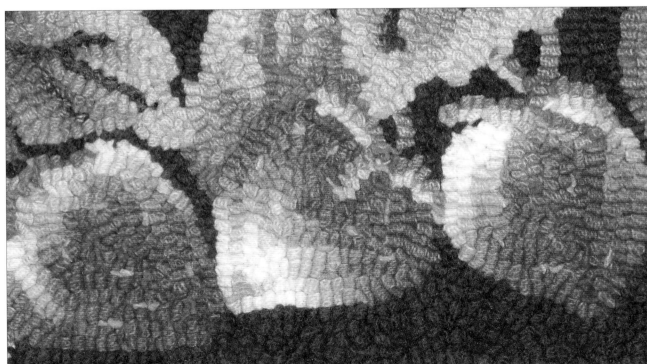

Detail, **Strawberry,** #4-cut dip dye wool and checked threads. Hooked by Norma Flodman.

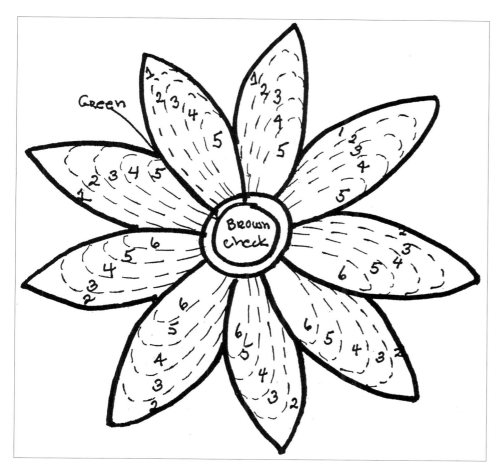

■ **Sunflower**—This is a great generic flower. It can be hooked with swatches, as shown in the diagram. It can be done with dip-dyes, going from a deep shade in the center and working to light on the edge. Sometimes I even like to dip the outer end in a touch of burgundy. An equally effective primitive method is to do each petal in a different shade of the same or similar color. With all versions, hook the center with a brown check or tweed. I like to outline that section with a medium shade of green.

Sunflower Pillow, #8-cut wool with swatches. Hooked by Susan Kievman.

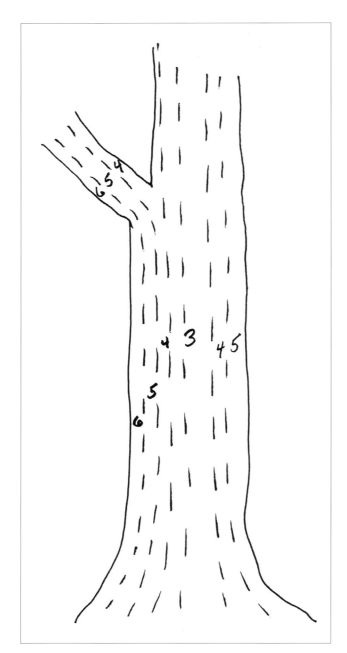

Two values of brown will give the impression of light filtering through the leaves to the upper branches of the tree. Two or three values of green can suggest a canopy of leaves—the lighter colors being used for leaves closer to the forefront with the darker ones to the rear. Dark values must also "define" the closer leaves, providing depth.

Detail, **The Bridge,** #3-cut wool. Hooked by Jane Olson. While this tree is much more detailed than the simple method described, it basically has one side that is darker than the other. The contrast between light and dark sections gives the tree some shape. Even the wiggly texture lines are darker on one side than on the other.

■ **Trees**—The simplest realistic tree to hook uses six values in vertical rows up the trunk. Start on the left side with the #6 value and work to #3 a little off center of the middle. Continue to the other side by going back to #4 and ending with #5, so the right side looks a bit lighter than the left.

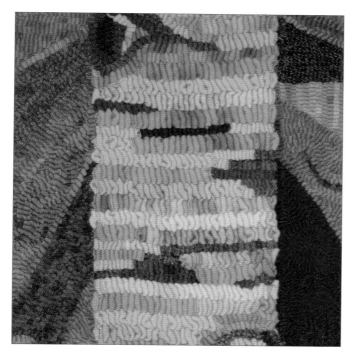

Birch trees are best hooked with horizontal lines. In this example white, natural, light gray, and assorted beige wools were used "as is" in cuts #8 and #10. The dark accent pieces were created by spot dying over the same "as is" wool and a few tweeds with Silver Gray, Plum and Mahogany. The rows were hooked with a bit of a dip in the middle to give a round feel to the trunk. Each outside edge has staggered ends to avoid a row of tails.

Detail, **Russian Birch.** Designed and hooked by Gene Shepherd, Anaheim, California. Change of cut size can help create distance when hooking trees. This photo shows five rows of trees, all hooked with the same wool. The closest tree was hooked with cuts #8 and #10. The tree on the left used #6, 5, and 4-cuts. Cuts #4 and #3 were used in the middle tree. These three trees were all hooked with horizontal rows in the same basic way. The back two rows were hooked in vertical rows. Of these two rows, #3 cut, with lighter wool was used for the closer line of trees. Hand-cut #2 beige wool was used for those trees at the greatest distance.

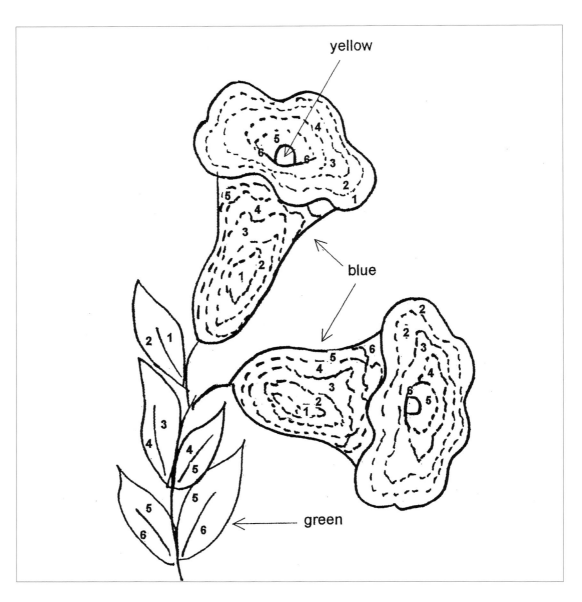

yellow

blue

green

■ Trumpet Flowers—

Whether hooking with swatches or scrap wool, follow the suggestions for light and dark sections as given in the diagram. Each method is equally easy to hook. These flowers come in so many colors: blue, lavender, white, yellow, pink and orange. They can also double as a padula model, letting you create your own variation as suits your needs.

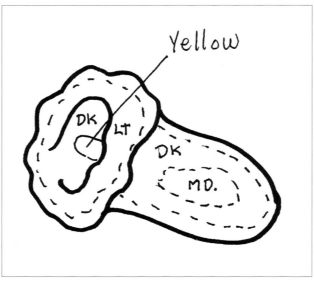

Yellow

DK

LT

DK

MD.

Primitive Trumpet Illustration. Rug hookers who prefer more "primitive" designs should learn to look at such directions, then run them through their wide cut processor, producing an image that looks like this.

Trumpet Flowers, #4- and 6-cut wool. Hooked by Iris Salter.

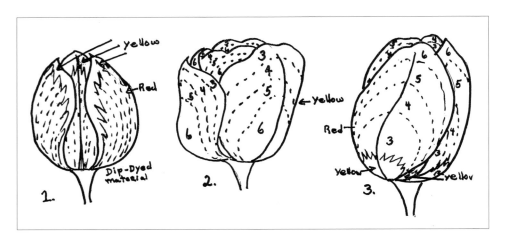

■ **Tulips**—Tulips come in such vivid colors that I only recommend you use four values, #3-6 cut, when using swatches. Follow the same guidelines for choosing colors if you want to do tulips with dip-dyes. These darker shades will help you keep the brilliance of your color. I have shown three ways to do tulips, but you can discover even more.

A #1 is for dip-dye, going red to yellow. Notice the petal is hooked in such a way that the yellow edge of the two main petals extends all the way to the base of the flower. This defines those petals, as well as allowing the center petal to be seen.

The #2 is for a dark to light tipped petal, using swatches. Be sure and hook the rounded contour of the petal so it will look natural. The light tips of the front petals are set off with the darker secondary colors of the next row.

And, #3 is similar to #2, but in reverse order of shade. Likewise, there is also a direction to add in a burst of different color at the very bottom.

Detail, **Tulips,** #4-cut wool with swatches. Hooked by Jane Olson.

■ **Turnovers**—Realistic leaves require some turnovers since all leaves do not lay flat. The most important thing to remember when working a turnover is to continue the shade of color around the edge of the turnover that is being used on the outside of the leaf. The under part of the leaf is always light. However, in some cases when the turnover is at the top of the leaf and you have used the lightest shade of color, hook the turnover in a dark shade.

There needs to be contrast. The larger the leaf, the more prominent the turnover, and the easier it is to hook. Assuming that green is being used for the leaves, try a different color of green for the turnover. This is very effective. The turnovers on leaves in a crewel rug pattern can be worked in entirely different colors. This makes the turnover and leaves outstanding. With the variety of colors hooked into fall leaves, you can really go wild on those turnovers.

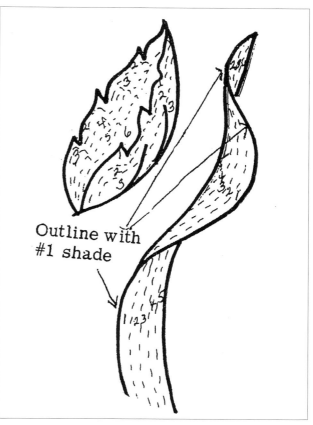

Outline with #1 shade

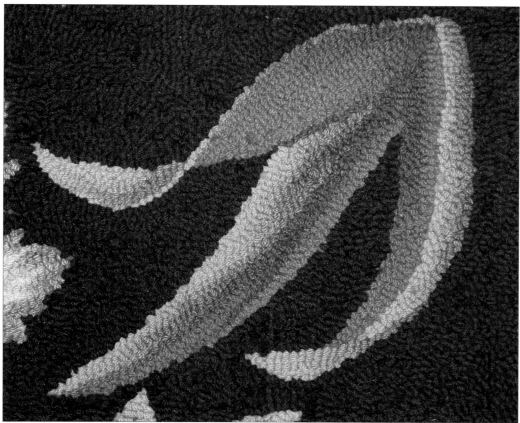

Detail, **Turnovers,** #4-cut dip dye wool Hooked by Jane Olson.

■ Umbrella—When hooking an umbrella think "half a pumpkin on a stick!" The ridges are the same. Directions for both shading and primitive versions are also the same.

Umbrella, #4-cut wool with swatch. Hooked by Jane Olson.

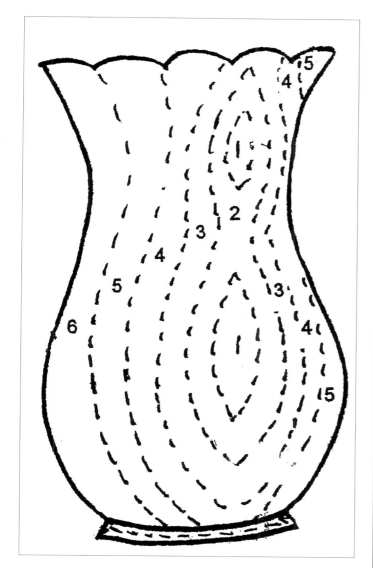

■ Vase—Vases are very simple to hook. As the diagram shows, the vase is darker on one side. It is shaded to the light past the center of the vase and then is shaded to a little darker on the right side of the vase. Highlights are a little off to one side, never exactly in the center. This same instruction applies to any shaped vase.

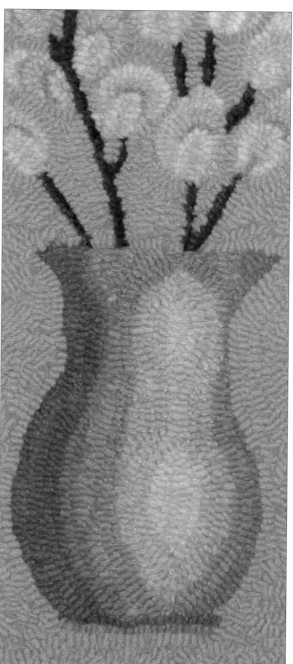

Detail, **Pussy Willow,** #3- and #4-cut wool. Hooked by Marguerite Ryan.

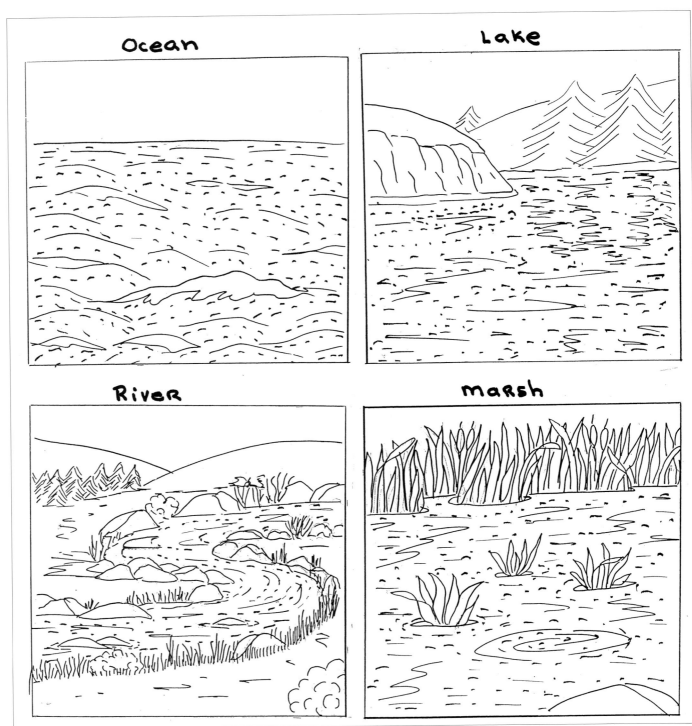

Ocean

Lake

River

marsh

■ **Water**—Even though you may be called upon to hook these four different kinds of water, all the wool needed can be dyed in just one process. Cut a piece of wool that is 3" by 18" from each of the following solid colors: white, natural, celery, light blue, light yellow, medium blue, pink and medium green. After soaking, place them in a large casserole pan of water and vinegar. Mix up ½ teaspoon of navy dye in one cup of boiling water and ½ teaspoon of turquoise dye

another cup of boiling water. Spoon spots of the navy dye and then the turquoise dye over the wool in the casserole pan. Use the spoon to press down the wool and diffuse the dye in the area so that it does not make harsh spots. As the wool starts to take up the dye, turn the wool pieces over and repeat the process. Do this several times until all the dye has been spotted over all the wool. When the wool has taken up the dye and all that is left is just a slight tint in the

Notice the wide variety of wool colors that this one dye bath will produce. These pieces will allow you to do the following kinds of water.

Detail from **The Ship,** #3-cut wool. Hooked by Jane Olson.

water, put in one more piece of white wool for just a few seconds. This will provide something to use for "white caps" in the ocean and river. Pure white is too strong used "as is." A moment in the weak dye bath will soften the white so that it will be just perfect.

■ **Brackish Water**—This type of still water usually looks best with the soft light grey–blue to tan colors the master dye bath will produce. Hook the rows in straight horizontal fashion, only adding rings at ripple points.

■ **Lake Water**—Lake water is composed of stronger colors than that used for the brackish water, since it reflects the colors of the sky. You should also reflect the colors of any trees or rocks on the shore line in the water. Do not repeat a mirror image of these objects. While you can use the same colors of the rocks and trees in the reflection, break up and distort the image with some additional turquoise lines. This shows movement in the water. Lakes are hooked in fairly straight horizontal rows with a little ripple here and there.

Detail, **Brackish Water.** Hooked by Jane Olson.

Detail, **Lake Water.** Hooked by Jane Olson.

- **River Water**—River water will need some of the brighter colors that came out of the master dye bath. You can also use the "white" wool for a little white water interest. Moving water like this will not reflect the trees or mountains.

- **Ocean Water**—The horizon in the ocean is always a straight line, with no movement. As you proceed to the foreground, the choppiness of the water will increase with more and more movement. You can make bigger "white caps" as you proceed to the foreground.

Detail, **River Water.** Hooked by Jane Olson.

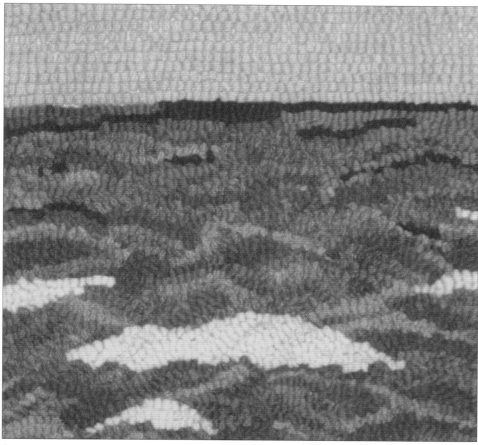

Detail, **Ocean Water.** Hooked by Jane Olson.

■ Water Lily—Water
lilies are very easy to hook
with either dip-dye or a
swatch. Whatever the
value of the bloom's base,
hook to the opposite value
at the tip of the petal. A
more primitive version
would be to outline with
either light or dark wool,
then fill with the other.
Water lilies typically come
in yellow, light green, blue
and pink.

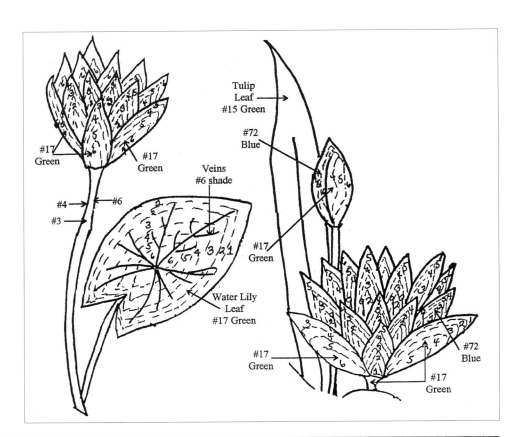

Detail, **Water Lily,** #4-cut wool. Hooked by Jane Olson.

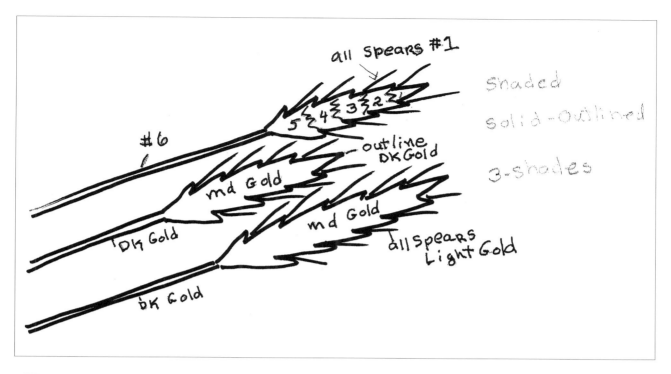

all spears #1

#6

Shaded
solid-outlined
3-shades

outline
DK Gold

md Gold

DK Gold

md Gold

all spears
Light Gold

DK Gold

5 4 3 2

■ **Wheat**—A mottled, 4-value lazy swatch is perfect for this design. (See Eggplant and Pumpkin for instructions on how to make one.) Of course, you can just use four values out of regular wheat colored swatch. Use your darkest choice for the stem and the first few kernels. The lightest value should be saved for the little wisps that come out of the kernels. The other two values can be used for the remaining kernels.

Detail, **Give Thanks Runner,** #4-cut wool with a 4-value lazy swatch. Hooked by Jane Olson.

Finishing Your Rug

CHAPTER 5

■ **Hooking the Edge**—Hooking the edge of your rug is very important, particularly when the rug has straight sides. Make sure that every loop is made in the same ditch so that the rug will be square. Corners can be achieved in any of the ways previously discussed, however, take extra care that none of your tails are made in such a way that they stick out of line. Edge loops should sit at a right angle to the direction of the edge.

■ **Blocking a Finshed Rug**—Blocking a finished rug is easy to do. When hooking is finished, if you have not done so already, sew a zigzag stitch on the backing, about one inch out from the hooked edge of the entire rug. Do not cut off any excess backing at this time.

Lay the rug upside down on a hard smooth surface that can take heat. Dining room tables are great for this if they are covered in heat blocking pads. A large piece of plywood will also work.

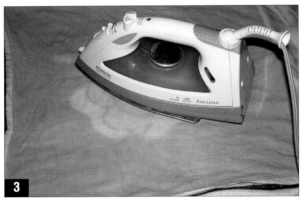

Starting in the center, press down a hot iron and allow the steam to penetrate the rug. When it stops sizzling, bring the iron up and press down in a wet section next slightly over from the last press. Place the iron, each time, with a straight down and straight up motion. Do not rub the iron over the rug like would be done for normal ironing. If there are sections that do not want to lay flat, repeat the process until they press down. It's normal to press the entire rug at least twice, rewetting the cloth in between. Stubborn sections and the outside edge may need an extra pressing or two.

Cover the back of the rug with a white cotton dish towel or piece of bed sheet that is wet.

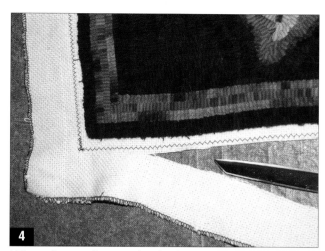

4

When the rug is completely dry, cut off the excess backing.

■ **Tweaking the Outside Edge**—The outside edge can be tweaked a bit if it is not as straight as desired. Press the section with an iron and wet cloth. Set the iron aside and gently pull on the excess backing as you coax the edge into shape. Re-steam immediately. If you can pull and steam at the same time, do so. Offending bulges on the edge can sometimes be pushed back into shape with a wooden straight edge—use a very thick yard stick for this. Once you've pushed or pulled to your satisfaction, cover with the wet cloth and steam the spot again to set. Allow the rug to stay in this position until dry. If the loops are particularly uneven, turn the rug over and repeat the steaming process on the front side as well.

Hooking the edge of your rug is very important, particularly when the rug has straight sides.

■ **Protecting the Edge**—Protecting the edge of your rug with the right finishing technique is very important. The edge is the most vulnerable part of any rug. One of the key ways to protect an edge is to limit it's availability to foot traffic. For that reason, never roll the edge around a piece of cording before whipping. It simply raises the edge so that it will be walked on. Our goal should be to whip the edge in such a way as to keep it below the surface of the loops. That allows the loops of the rug to evenly take the foot wear, not the edge. Some people like to fold the rug backing before whipping or place unused strips of wool under the tape. Again, all this does is raise a section of the rug so that it will prematurely wear out. If you would like to test this advice, place a pencil under a rug that gets heavy foot traffic. In just a few months time, that spot will start to wear differently than the rest of the rug. Don't do anything to the edge that will cause it to stick up any higher than necessary.

STRAIGHT EDGES #101

Getting a good, straight edge on your rug begins with the way the pattern is drawn on your backing. Before you ever begin to hook, make sure the four straight sides to your pattern run "in the ditch" created by the rows of holes in your backing. If the pattern is not drawn straight, redraw the pattern so that it is.

Although we usually work from the center out to the edge of a rug, hook the outside edge perimiter line earlier in the process. By hooking two rows all the way around your rug, you can establish a good border as well as have something to which you can hook up to.

■ Whipping the Edge—Whipping the edge with 4-ply yarn provides maximum protection for the edge.

Fold over the 1" wide backing at the first row of hooking. Jane can just fold it and sew; Gene needs to pin it down. Using a large dull needle and 4-ply yarn, whip a finished edge around the rug. Choose any color you wish. Jane uses a single strand of acrylic yarn. Gene likes a double strand of wool yarn. In this photo, the yarn was "started" by basting it through a section of the linen backing. An inch or so is enough to hold it in place. If you match the yarn to the border edge, the yarn will be nearly invisible. Sometimes a contrasting color from another section of the rug will give just a hint of spice to the edge.

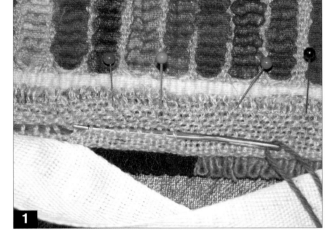

After basting, bring the needlepoint to one side or another and push it through the first hole. Go right through a hole that already has a loop in it. Since Jane sews through the back to the front and Gene sews from the front to the back, it probably does not make any difference which side you choose. It does matter that you pull the yarn through so that it snugs up. Bring the needlepoint back to the starting side and repeat. When the yarn runs out, simply baste an inch or two of the ending piece in the backing like was done to begin. Do not knot! Start a new piece of yarn in the backing by basting and then continue whipping as before.

The whipped edge should be nice and tight like this.

■ **Threading your Needle**—Trouble threading your needle with yarn? Try this tip. Fold a piece of yarn over the needle and hold both ends below, creating some pressure on the fold. Pull the yarn tightly over the needle so that it eventually rides down the edge, popping the needle out. That kinked section of yarn will now easily push through the eye of the needle.

■ **Mitering a Corner**—A mitered corner will make a cleaner edge. It takes very little effort to do this before the edge is whipped. However, it makes a big difference in the way the finished product looks.

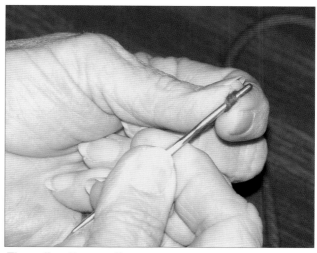

Threading the needle.

Fold the corner in and pin.

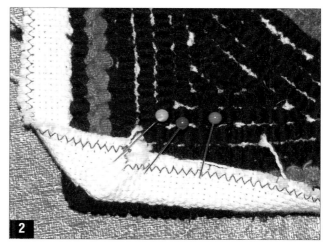

Fold over side #1 and pin.

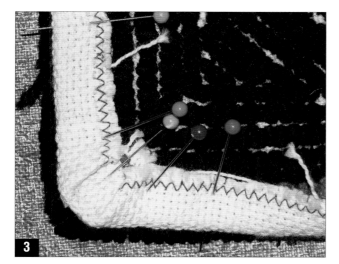

Fold over side #2 and pin.

Take the time to miter the rug tape as well as the backing. Besides sewing down the inner edge of the rug tape, sew together the mitered corner. It's worth the effort as it makes the piece look professional.

■ **Whipping again**—After the entire rug is whipped with yarn, cover the exposed rug backing with cotton rug tape and whip the outside edge of the tape to the yarn edge with heavy duty thread. Then, whip the inside edge down with thread, so that the rug tape lies flat. When sewing the inside edge, make sure to catch the thread in the little bare spots of backing, not the underneath side of the loops. Sewing to the loops will eventually cause them to pull out.

■ **Saving a Step**—You can save a step by sewing through the rug tape at the same time the edge is being whipped.

It's done in the same way as already described, except that, after folding over the backing, lay the tape on and pin it all together. That way the backing and tape can both be whipped in one pass with the yarn. The only sewing to do with thread is for the inner edge.

If the rug is to be hung, a second piece of tape can also be layered over the first before it is whipped with yarn. By doing this at the top and bottom, rod pockets can be created as a part of the edge. This evenly distributes the weight across the entire top edge, as well as gives enough bottom weight to hang straight.

■ **Adding Fringe**—Fringe can be added to hooked rugs. To do so, first whip the entire edge with yarn as described above. Then go back and sew the fringe to the underneath side of the rug, making sure to catch the backing in the hooked areas. Carefully attach the fringe to the topside of the rug by sewing into the yarn. This will keep the fringe

from pulling away from the rug. Finally, sew the rug tape on the underneath side, so that it will protect both edges of the rug and fringe tape.

■ **Never Seal**—Never paint the back of a hooked rug with rubberized latex sealer. It ruins the value of the rug. It makes it impossible to repair should it ever be damaged. It keeps the rug from breathing. It gets crumbly with use and is just, overall, disgusting. We will fine you if we ever come to your house and discover that you did this to one of your wonderful hand hooked rugs!

■ **Maintaining Floor Rugs**—Maintaining floor rugs is made easier when they are situated in appropriate spots. Choose a place where the rug will be used, not abused. The entry doorway, where people constantly track in mud, is probably not the best spot to put a hand hooked rug. For most people, the kitchen or toilet areas are other good places to avoid. When chair or table legs are constantly moved back and forth on the same spot of a hooked rug there is a good chance that holes will develop at that spot. Still, don't be afraid to put rugs in normal traffic areas. When using them on a hard surface, place them on a thin rubber non skid mat. This provides a little cushion to the rug, as well as helping it to not move when being walked on. People successfully use their rugs everyday in most living areas of their homes. Wool rugs on a good linen or cotton backing are strong and dirt resistant. They often can be used for decades with out any special care at all.

■ **Cleaning a Hooked Rug**—Cleaning a hooked rug is something that should be done sparingly, and then by hand. Most spills can be spot cleaned with water and a little white vinegar or a weak solution of Woolite. Do not take hooked rugs to a dry cleaner.

Should the entire rug need a deep cleaning, place it upside down in a bath of lukewarm water with a weak Woolite solution. Gently move the rug a little, coaxing out the dirt. Drain out the dirty water and refill with tepid water. Again, gently move the rug a bit, coaxing out more dirt. Repeat this until the water remains clean. You may have to do this several times. After the final draining, roll the rug up in a terry towel and gently squeeze as much water out of the rug as possible. Lay it out on a surface and block with a hot iron as would be done for a new rug. Pick a place where it can be left to dry without being disturbed. Sometimes if the rug is really thick, it might take as much as two or three days for this. A spot directly under a ceiling fan is perfect as the moving air will speed up the drying process. Directional fans also help with this. It's good to flip the rug over every four or five hours so drying can take place on both sides. .

If the rug is too big for the tub, place it on a large piece of plastic film in your driveway. Gently work a Woolite solution through the rug, brushing in the same direction from one end to the other, using a very soft brush or rolled up terry towel. If it needs more work, repeat the procedure working in another direction. Rinse with the hose, and then blot out as much water as possible with terry towels. Drying a rug like this is a problem as it holds a lot more moisture than a smaller rug. Don't be tempted to leave it out in the sun all day. The sun's direct rays are not good for dyed wool rugs. Even a protected place outside is not perfect as the rug will attract dew during the night. A dry, clean place, like a garage, basement or family room floor is the best option. Direct as many fans as possible on the rug and carefully turn it every so often until it is dry.

If you live in the snow belt, let nature clean your rugs. After a fresh snow, lay the rug face side down on a clean spot. Leave it there a few hours. The snow will pull the dirt out of the rug. Bring the rug back in the house, block it as described and then let it dry over night. This works for both hooked and braided wool rugs.

■ **Repairing a Damaged Rug**—Repairing a damaged rug is a difficult and time-consuming project. If the damaged rug is on a burlap foundation, chances are that it is only going to continue deteriorating. That means, even if it is repaired, it should either be hung on the wall or placed in an area where it is never walked on.

1. If your heirloom rug is just beginning to fray at the edge and you intend to hang it on the wall, sometimes you can just rip out a row or two from the outside border, fold the old burlap and whip again. This will allow you to hang the rug for several more years.

2. If damage is more extensive—most of the edge is gone and there are interior holes completely through the rug—the old rug must be secured to a new backing. Cut a piece of new backing at least 6" larger than the old rug. Do not complicate the problems by using burlap. Choose something that will hold up over time, like monk's cloth or linen. Lay the old rug on the new backing and then tack the old rug to the new backing with a heavy thread. Go between the rows of hooking at regular intervals so that the two pieces are secured. Then, in the same way, sew around any holes or particularly worn sections of the rug. If the edge is to be repaired, rip out a couple of rows until there is enough backing that is strong enough to be sewn down. Sew around the entire edge of the rug. Be sure to save any wool that is ripped out while doing this procedure.

3. After the old rug is securely sewn to a new backing, hooking can commence. Hook as usual except when ever possible, hook through both the old and new backing. All the old wool strips, which were removed can be reused. For those sections where the wool is completely gone, do the best job that you can to match. All of this takes a great deal of time, but if the rug is a family heirloom and well hooked, it is worth all the trouble. Once repaired, put it in a safe spot that receives little traffic.

CAUTION: HOOKED RUGS & WATER MAY NOT MIX!

If the dyed wool in your hooked rug was not properly "set" the colors may run when the rug comes in contact with water. Certain colors, like red, sometimes run even when they have been set. Before attempting a major washing job, it's always a good idea to wet just a corner first to see what happens. You may prefer to "put up" with a dirty rug rather than one where the colors have all run toegther. Serious washing should only be use for extreme situations that are worth the risk.

CHAPTER 6

Hooking Special Projects

BRICK DOOR STOPS

Brick Door Stop, #6-cut of wool. Hooked by Norma Flodman.

Brick doorstops are simple to hook and make great little gifts. When planning a project like this, make sure your brick is 8" x 4" x 2¹/₄". Each doorstop will take a little less than ¹/₄ yard of material. If using left over wool, the sides can even be hooked in different colors. If you use synthetic homespun for a backing, the background does not have to hooked at all.

After hooking, pinch each corner together and whip with a complimentary wool yarn on the outside corner edge.

When all four corners are sewn, fold all the corners back against a side. Fold all of them in the same direction, like to the right, so no two corners of excess fabric overlap. Push the brick down into the fabric box.

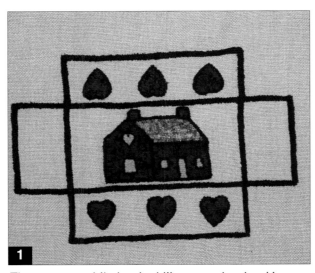

1

The pattern, while hooked like any other hooking project, must be sized and shaped like this so it will fit around the brick. Synthetic homespun was used for this project, negating the need for any background hooking.

3

Overlap the backside of the brick as neatly as possible. Fold everything down and sew it together.

If the backing is not large enough to completely cover the bottom of the brick, cut a piece of thick wool the size of the bottom rectangle, (8" x 4") and baste it to the outer edge.

CHAIR PAD

Jane Olson Sat Here, 13" diameter. #6-cut wool on monk's cloth. Designed and hooked by Gene Shepherd.

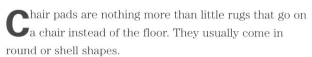

Tea Time, #10-cut wool selvages on monk's cloth. Designed and hooked by Gene Shepherd. Thick wool selvages in a #10-cut make a comfortable shell shaped pad.

Gene finishes his chair seats exactly as he would a rug and then sits them on a non stick rubber mat cut a bit smaller than the finished pad. It provides both cushion and a non-skid service.

Chair pads are nothing more than little rugs that go on a chair instead of the floor. They usually come in round or shell shapes.

If the chair pad is intended for a specific spot, make a template that perfectly fits the bottom of that chair. Do this by folding a piece of stiff paper—brown paper bags work well—and cut it in the shape of the chair bottom. Trace the shape as the outside edge for the design. If you already have a round commercial seat pattern, super-impose the shape over the design and proceed.

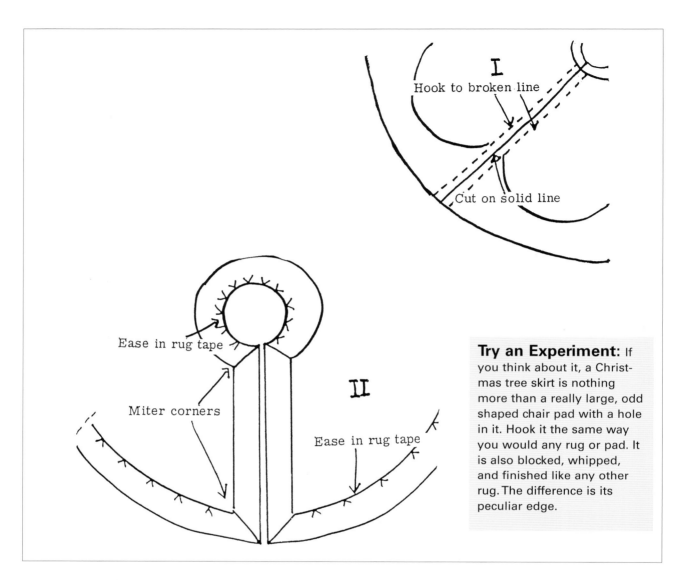

Hook to broken line

I

Cut on solid line

Ease in rug tape

Miter corners

II

Ease in rug tape

Try an Experiment: If you think about it, a Christmas tree skirt is nothing more than a really large, odd shaped chair pad with a hole in it. Hook it the same way you would any rug or pad. It is also blocked, whipped, and finished like any other rug. The difference is its peculiar edge.

Call Norma for a Good Time, Designed and hooked by Gene Shepherd, #6 cut wool on monk's. Chair seats make great little gifts that can help you connect with friends.

Jane finishes a chair seats in exactly the same way that she finishes a rug, with one exception. After whipping the edge with wool she does not apply rug tape. Instead, she cuts a round of wool, a little bigger than the chair seat round shape. After folding over the edge of the wool piece, it is whipped to the edge of the seat. This provides a little extra padding, as well as a finished looking bottom.

Since round rugs will always have extra backing when the edge is folded over to whip, it's a good idea to cut some notches out of the excess backing before whipping. To do this for anything that is rounded, zigzag a "V" at regular intervals around the curved portion of the extra backing. Before folding and whipping, cut out the "Vs." This allows the folded section to lie flatter. It's similar to the "notches" called for in clothing construction.

PILLOW

Leaf Sampler, 14", #5-cut ordered pancake wool on monk's cloth. Hooked by Gene Shepherd. Pillows are great as decorative accents or a significant gift when you don't have the time or inclination to do a complete rug!

A pillow top is hooked exactly like a rug. Since it won't be walked on, you can use a variety of accent fibers that would not be good for a floor rug. Once hooked, the pillow is steamed and prepared for finishing exactly like a rug.

Jane likes to whip her edge with wool, and then sew the hooked portion to a backing, which has been prepared to fit the finished pillow top.

Cut your backing about 2" bigger than your finished pillow size. Fold over a 1" edge all the way around the backing and press with a hot iron. Be sure to miter the corners. Carefully pin the backing to the pillow and sew with thread.

After three sides are sewn together, stuff the interior with a pillow form. Jane cuts hers from upholstery foam. Once in place, the last edge is whipped. Usually, she makes a yarn rope edge to tack on the seam.

Gene prepares the backing in exactly the same way, but he whips through the backing and the pillow top at the same time.

While the pillow is empty, it is easy to pin the two pieces together before whipping with wool yarn.

If there is a "bottom" to the pillow, start whipping about $1^1/2$" away from a corner on what would be the bottom. Whip the $1^1/2$" to the corner and turn, whipping as you go. Whip all three complete sides. Keep another $1^1/2$" past the final. This will provide an open section on the bottom side of the pillow, which is big enough to slip in the stuffing. Gene usually stuffs the pillow with a feather or down bed pillow that easily condenses into the size of the smaller pillow.

Once the filling is in place, pinch or pin together the two sections and continue whipping until done. This section is usually more difficult to whip. That's why it's good for it to be on the bottom.

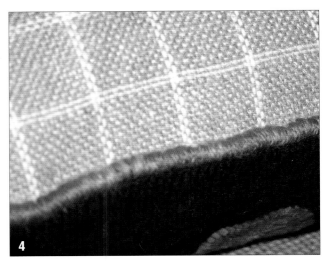

4

Use wool yarn, doubled, to make a good edge.

Finishing options for pillows are limited to your own creativity. There is no end to alternative ways of finishing pillows. Here are just a few:

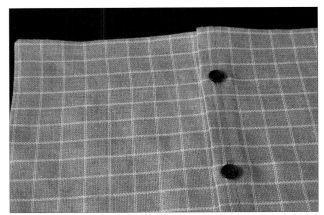

If you have sewing skills, you might want to make a backing of two hemmed pieces, which are buttoned together. This will allow the pillow to be removed.

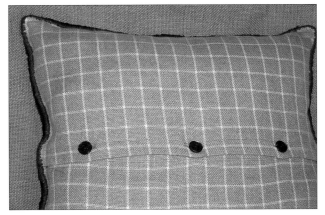

This makes an attractive finished product. However, it is more difficult to sew together.

Anna Boyer included a beaded fringe between her layers when finishing this pillow.

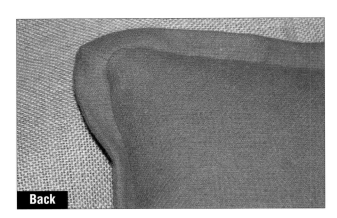

Back

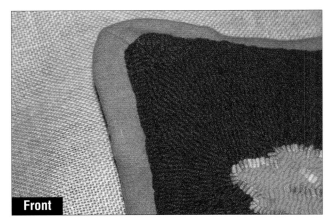

Front

Jean Coon brought her wool pillow backing around to the front side—creating a different look.

ROPE EDGING

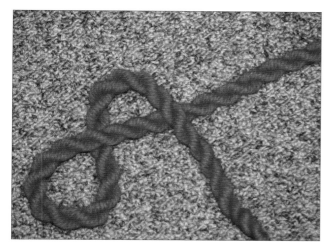

Rope edging is very easy to make. It provides a convenient way to simplify your finishing techniques for pillows and other hooked pieces.

If you need 5' of rope, measure 15' with an upright at each end.

Tie the fiber to one of the uprights. Stretch the fiber to the other stationary point, wrap around, and come back. Do several rotations. If mixing fibers, do a complete rotation or two before tying off the first fiber at point #1 and tying in the new. It's easier to do complete rotations, always adding in new strands at the same place. The number of rotations depends on the thickness of the fiber being used and the desired rope thickness needed. If using an average weight yarn, go around the markers at least five or six times.

Once the fiber has been wound, tie off the end at the beginning point. While that point may have knots and loose ends, the other point, 15' way, should just have fibers neatly wrapped around the marker. If six rotations were made, then there would be six fibers coming to the point and six fibers going around and back to the other chair. All these spans should be the same length—no sagging lines.

At the smooth turn, separate the two sides by "hooking" in between the fibers with your finger. Lift them up off the stationary object so they can be twisted.

Jane sells a handy little "egg beater" type tool that has a hook instead of beaters. Place the hooked section of the fibers on the tool's hook and start turning. Without this tool, a variable speed drill will also work. Use a few strands of heavy plastic electrician's tape to hook between the fibers at the turn. Securely tape the fibers to a drill bit sticking out of the drill. Make sure there is at least 3" of heavy tape between the turn and the drill. Without Jane's egg beater or a power drill you can use any sort of rigid hook that has enough of a shaft to hold as you turn. However, it's not nearly as much fun to do it this way as using a power tool!

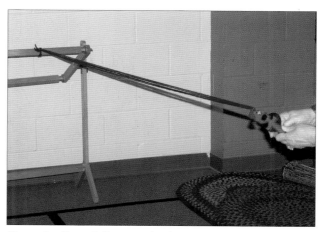

Keep the lines fully stretched as you begin to twist.

More twisting is better than less. This is one of those times when it is better to do more than less. All the fibers need to twist down into a single tight strand. If you are working with a 15' span and hope to produce a 5' rope, then you will want to twist that 15' span down to about an 11 or 12' length. You will need to gradually move towards the other stationary point as you twist since the span will get shorter.

Cut the secured ends off and immediately tie them into one big knot so that the rope can not unwind.

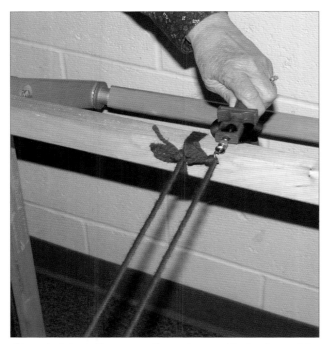

Once twisted, the opposite ends need to be brought together without lessening the tension on the twisted cord. Get a helper to hold the cord in the center while the two ends are moved together. In lieu of another person, put another chair at that spot so it can hold the center as the cord wraps around it. Be sure to keep a tension on the cord while you do this.

After the twisted cord is folded with both ends together at one end, have the helper let go of the bended end. It will spring to life and double back on itself in a rope form. If it is not completely uniform in its formation, you can play with it a bit to improve the shape.

A rope edging can be done in any color of yarn or other fibers you like. It makes a great addition to a pillow edge or even handles for handbags. Should you want tassels at the corners of your pillow, make a loop of rope at each corner as you tack the rope around the perimeter. The starting and stopping corner will end up with both tails of the rope. Use some additional yarn to tightly wrap around the rope at the twist. Tie and hide the ends in the knot. Cut the end and you have a tassel at each corner.

Nutcracker, 14" high, #3-cut and #4-cut. Hooked by Peggy Johnson. Three-dimensional stand ups work well for "doll-like" designs. The figure will need both a hooked front and back.

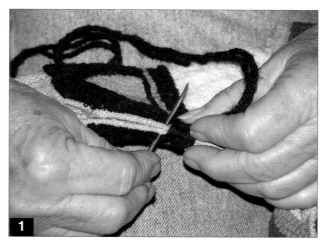

Once hooked, the two pieces are whipped together just as would be done for a pillow. Be sure to leave the bottom open.

Taking a little time to use wool that matches each of the hooked sections will produce a very professional look.

Find a plastic bottle with a screw down top that will fit inside the figure. Fill it with cat litter and screw on the top. Pad the bottle and place it inside the figure.

Cut a round piece of wool that is one inch larger than the bottom opening of the figure. Fold in ½" on the wool round and whip it to the hooked figure.

When finished, the bottom should be smooth and neat.

Snowman, 14" high, #3 and #4-cut wool. Designed by Jane Olson. Hooked by Iris Salter.

Try an Experiment: If you think about it, a Christmas Stocking is an odd shaped version of the "stand up" just described. Two pieces— both could be hooked or one hooked and the other a piece of fabric—are whipped together just like they were with the stand up, creating a bag or stocking. Instead of filling with a bottle and sewing a round of fabric over the opening, why not just finish the edge and make a stocking? It could be lined or unlined.

FLOWER PINS

This is an easy project. It's also a great way to make little gifts using up leftover scraps of wool and backing. They can be used as accessories on clothing, hats, or packages. To do this project you will need scrap wool and backing, craft glue, a credit card, rubber bands, stiff craft felt, "broach style" pins for the back, paper clips, hole punch, and hot glue gun.

Flower Pin

Place a piece of backing on your frame. Hook a regular cat's paw for the center of a flower. It can be oval or round. Of the centers pictured, one was surrounded with medium high loops, another with two levels of high loops and the third with prodded petals. Be sure and leave about 2$^1/_2$"– 3" between each flower. Make as many as you can without repositioning your backing. All flowers should be at least 2" away from the edge of your frame.

Take a credit card "squeegee" and smooth the glue out around the flower, right up to but not on the hooked petals. The glue must be forced down into the weave of the backing. Each flower should have at least a $^1/_2$" border of smoothed glue around it. Make sure not to rub any glue over the edge of the frame. Let this project sit on your frame for at least an hour, or until the fabric is completely dry.

When finished hooking, pull all the petals of each flower together and secure with a rubber band. Make sure they can't shake loose. Next, run a bead or two of white craft glue around each flower.

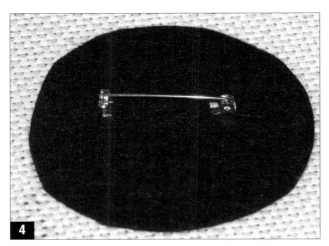

While the glue dries, cut rounds of stiff craft felt. These should be a little bigger than the cat's paw center of each flower.

Measure the "broach style" pins—they have a flat base that bends up on each end. This example had a flat base of 1". Punch two holes, an inch a part, in the felt round. Slip the necks of the pin through their respective holes and fasten the clasp. You'll need one round per flower.

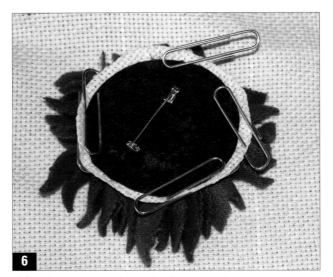

Glue the felt rounds to the backs of the flowers. While either white craft glue or a hot glue gun will do this, the hot glue works much quicker. Make sure that the pin back side of the felt rests against the bottom of the hooked flower—the pin arm must be on the outside so that it can operate. Pinch felt and flower together so that it adheres. If using glue, paperclip the edges and let the piece dry for an additional time. Wool leaves can also be added to the back if you would like. When completely dry, trim off any excess.

When the glue around the flowers is completely dry, take the backing off the frame. The glued sections should be very stiff. Cut between the flowers. Round the base of each flower so that it is approximately the size of the felt already cut.

HANGING A RUG

A rug, properly displayed, will hang as straight and even as possible. This can be accomplished several ways.

Tip 1: The easiest way is to put extra rug tape or some other kind of fabric at the top and the bottom of the backside, so that a sleeve is created at each end. Decorative rods can go in both, giving enough weight for the rug to hang straight. If you don't want the rods to show at the bottom, just use dowels slightly smaller than the rug. If the rug is more than 3' long there needs to be a middle support for the rod. Cut a little hole in the backside of the sleeve so a wall bracket can fit in to support the rod. Spans longer than 3' tend to eventually sag.

Tip 2: Cut a piece of $1/4$" plywood slightly smaller than the size of your finished piece. Cover the front side and edges of the plywood with material the same color as the rugs background or edge. Tack the rug to the plywood with small brad nails. These will not show and will hold the rug firmly in place. The piece can then be hung as one would hang a picture frame. Just make sure that the wall hangers used are strong enough to handle the weight of the plywood.

Tip 3: Prefabricated carpet strips that are used for professional carpet installation can also support a hooked rug on the wall. Cut four pieces that will make a frame slightly smaller than the rug you wish to hang. Nail them to wall with finishing nails, making sure that the little tacks on the strip point out. A rug will easily stretch over the frame and can be removed and then reinstalled with no problems.

HOW TO DRAW A RECTANGLE OR SQUARE

1. When making a rectangle pattern, you will, of course, draw the rectangle on your paper pattern. However, in this case, do not use the paper rectangle as a guide to draw it on the backing of your pattern. The material cannot be laid straight enough to coincide exactly with the ditch. Use the paper pattern to get your measurements, and then find the appropriate ditches on the backing of the actual pattern. For discussion, we will be making a rectangle pattern, 2' by 3'.

2. Cut the backing 8" longer and wider than the finished pattern, or 2' 8" by 3' 8". Finish the edge so that it will not unravel.

3. Measure in 4" from any side and mark that ditch. Use a permanent marker to draw a line, precisely in that ditch, until you come close to the edge of the backing.

4. Once again, at the edge you just approached, measure in 4" and find the second ditch, which will run at a right angle to the first line. Mark in that ditch until you have gone the length of the side. You should have intersected with the first line, creating a right angle composed of a 3' line and a 2' line.

5. Smooth the backing out as flat as possible without distorting it. Using the short line as your edge, measure over to find the parallel ditch exactly 3' away. Do the same thing from the first long line to find the parallel line exactly 2' away. Follow those two new marks to finish off the rectangle.

6. Once you have used the ditches to define your rectangle on the backing, the rest of the pattern can be transferred within the rectangle that you have drawn. Squares are made in exactly the same way.

HOW TO DRAW AN OVAL

1. Decide the finished size that is wanted for your project. This diagram is for a 3' x 5' finished rug. That means the backing will have to be 8" wider and longer in order to give you enough extra on the outside of the pattern.

2. Choose a work surface that is both big enough to hold your drawing and capable of sustaining a nail hole. A sheet of plywood is perfect. Your dining room table is not.

3. Cut a piece of good quality paper at least as big as the backing you will end up with—3' 8" by 5' 8" in this case. At right angles, drawn two lines at the center of your paper, one 3" and the other 5", which intersect in the exact middle of each. Tack down the corners of the paper so that it is smooth and flat.

4. Subtract the width from the length. In this case, 5" minus 3" is 2, or 24".

5. Divide that amount by 4, which gives the number 6.

6. Measure in 6" from each end of the length. At that point, nail or push a heavy tack or sturdy nail.

7. Cut and tie a string loop that will be long enough to go around both nails and extend past the second nail precisely to the 5' edge mark. Make sure to use some sort of heavy twine that will not stretch. Yarn, for example will not work for this because it stretches too much and will distort the shape.

8. Insert a pencil in this loop at the outermost edge. Holding the pencil vertical, draw a line very slowly, keeping the string very taunt. If the string slips off the pencil, just replace it. Draw the line completely around the paper. You now have

a perfect oval measuring 3' by 5'. Go over the line with a marker. Put a little mark at the A, B, C, D, and X points.

9. Transferring the oval to your backing can be a tricky process because backings can stretch. Lay the backing on the pattern, smooth it out as straight as possible and pin it at points A, B, C, D, and X. Follow the ditch from point A to B, making sure the pin at each end is in the same ditch. Make sure the very center of the pattern, point X, is also pinned in this ditch. From X, follow the intersecting ditch up to point C and pin. Then, follow the ditch back down to X and then on to D and pin. A and B will be in the same ditch and C and D will be in the same ditch. X is where both ditches intersect. Using additional pins at regular intervals around the pattern will stabilize everything so that you get a good oval.

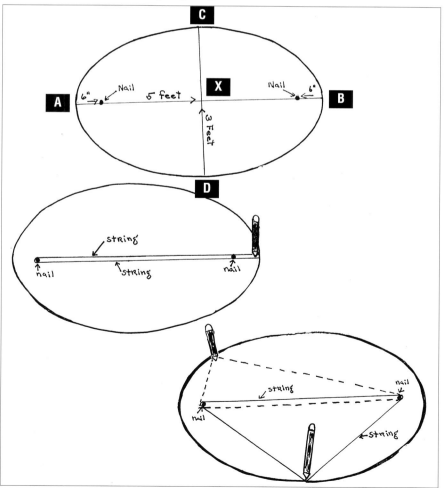

Oval Illustration

HOW TO DRAW A LARGE CIRCLE

1. Determine the size circle you want. Take that size and divide by two. If a circle 36" wide is desired, then the number would be 18".

2. Choose a work surface that is both big enough to hold the pattern and sustain a nail hole. A sheet of plywood is perfect. Your dining room table is not.

3. Cut a piece of good quality paper at least 8" bigger than the size of the finished circle. In this case it would be 44" square. Secure it to your workspace so it will not slip. Draw two 36" lines so that they intersect at a perfect right angle.

4. In the center of the paper, drive a sturdy 2" long finishing nail.

5. Take a straight thin piece of wood, like a yardstick, and measure two spots exactly 18" apart. At those spots, drill a small hole. Using a measuring stick makes this easy. Drill the hole on the 1" mark and the 19" mark, a perfect 18" span. String can also be used to do this; however, string always stretches and makes it very hard to get an exact circle. The wood will not stretch.

6. Place one hole over the nail. Stick a pencil in the second hole. Hold it upright and carefully draw the circle. Make a little mark at points A, B, C, D, and X.

7. To transfer, follow the instructions for transferring an oval given in point 9. While it will take a bit more time to pin the backing to the pattern, the effort will be worth it.

Small Circles, 14" and down, can be achieved with much less work. While they can easily be drawn on paper with a compass, transferring that exact shape to rug backing without any distortion can be a problem. Gene suggests finding something in the kitchen that is exactly the size you want. "My 13" standard round chair seat shape is exactly the size of my wife's missing cake plate … get the picture?" If you need a circle exactly 3½" across and aren't open to giving up kitchen utensils, take your ruler to a thrift shop and start measuring. It really is the easiest way to get small, precise circles. By pressing down on a beverage glass, bowl or lid, it exerts pressure around the whole perimeter, helping to reduce movement of the backing while you draw. (By the way, the cake plate info is just between you and me – hooker to hooker.)

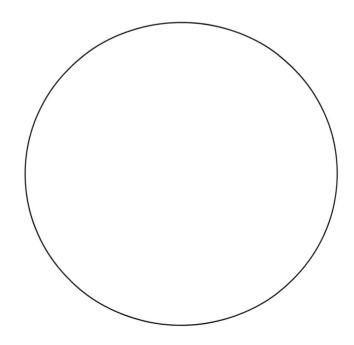

CHAPTER 7

Jane Olson on Her Soap Box

Most of these quotes come straight from the pages of
The Rugger's Roundtable. The rest, vintage Olson all, are things she just
hasn't had time to put in the newsletter.

JANE OLSON ON DYEING WOOL

I am amazed at the new information about dyeing! It is becoming more complicated than it actually is for the average rug hooker. So much time is spent on preparing and dyeing that it takes the joy out of the craft.

■ **Before dyeing,** pre-soak your wool in hot water with a little liquid detergent until it is thoroughly wet. This only takes about 5 minutes if you are using 100% wool flannel. Other wool, that may have been treated with water repellents will, at the most, take 15 minutes to soak. Do not worry about rinsing the soapy water out of the material. This has no effect one way or another when dyeing.

■ **To start dyeing,** measure your dry dye into a measuring cup. Pour in 1 cup of boiling water and mix well. Next, measure the amount of liquid dye solution you want to use and pour it in to simmering water. You will need enough water to thoroughly cover whatever amount of wool you want to dye. Mix well. Add $1/4$ to $1/2$ cup of white vinegar or mordant of your choice. I like white vinegar because it is cheap and readily available at any market regardless of where I am. I buy it by the case.

■ **The water in the dye pot needs to be on a low simmer.** You do not

want the water to be at a rolling boil—just a bubble now and then.

■ **If you want a solid, even color,** add hot soaked wool to the dye pot and stir constantly for five minutes. If the material still looks blotchy after five minutes, even though you have stirred the material constantly, add more liquid detergent to the dye bath. This will not interfere with the dye. It will make the material more porous, soften the water, and allow the material to absorb the dye more evenly.

■ **If you want a mottled effect,** stir just enough to distribute the dye through all of the wool—about 15-20 seconds. It will take about 20 minutes for most dyes to set. If you

want a slightly mottled effect stir it occasionally over the 20 minutes. If you want more mottling, do not stir again.

■ **The water in the dye bath will turn clear when the wool "takes up" the dye and "sets."** Some dye colors do clear up better than others. Reds can be particularly difficult. If the water doesn't seem to be clearing up after 20 minutes, try turning up the heat. That usually helps. Don't go off and leave the pot unattended as it's very easy to over boil, and thus felt, your wool.

■ **If there is still some color in the dye water,** it means that the wool reached its maximum absorption level. Instead of throwing the water

The Shepherd back yard on dyeing day.

away, put in another piece of wool with a little vinegar. It can always be used for something later on.

■ **When the material is dyed, rinse it in cold water.** This does not felt the material! What shrinks the material to a felt stage is either over boiling it in the dye pot or over agitating it in the washing machine when trying to rinse it. Cold water does not harm the hot wool.

■ **I like to rinse my newly dyed wool in the washing machine.** When dyeing a lot of wool, I fill my washing machine with cold water and stop the cycle. When my different pieces are done, I drain them and then put them right into the washer. When I am through dyeing, or have a full load, I let the machine agitate for about 45 seconds and then move it to the spin dry cycle.

■ **To dry wool,** hang it on the clothesline or place in the dryer with a couple of bath towels. Check it every so often and remove when dry.

■ **All wool shrinks** when dyed in hot water. I have found that I lose about 2" in every yard I dye.

■ **Old wool clothing and material can be recycled for hooked rugs.** Remove the linings, buttons and zippers first, and then wash the material in warm water and liquid detergent on a short delicate cycle. This clothing has solvent and water repellent in it from many visits to the dry cleaner. Once clean, you can over-dye these pieces or use as is.

■ **When dyeing a new formula,** only pour half the dye mixture into the dye pot. You can always add more dye if the shade is too light. This way you have not dyed a color or shade that is too dark for your use.

■ **When spot dyeing,** soak your wool in hot water and vinegar before you start. Lay the material on a large pan and pour the different colors you are using over the material about 2" apart here and there. You can either simmer the spotted wool in water for 20 minutes or wrap with aluminum foil and bake for 30 minutes at 300 degrees.

■ **When spot dyeing and the spot is too strong,** immediately pour clear hot water over the area and this will rinse off some of the dye before it sets.

■ **When spot dyeing for fall leaves,** I like to mix up five different colors, each in a $1/2$ cup of boiling water. I use $1/8$ of a teaspoon each of bronze green, rust, orange, bold and seal brown. I like to spoon the dyes over colored wool—medium brown, medium green, orange, gold and rust materials. You can use all or just some of the colors on each piece of wool. When using more than one color, they blend as they run together, giving you a wonderful finished project.

My favorite spot dyes are:
■ Green, Plum and Orange over tan or bronze green wool.
■ Olive Green, Old Rose and Plum over beige, aqua or gray wool.
■ Bright Green, Old Rose or Golden Brown over beige, gray blue, and gold wool.

■ **When a piece you've just dyed has one white thread,** it probably means that the manufacturer has included a synthetic thread in the warp of your 100% wool.

■ **When you want to remove dye from a piece of wool,** bring a kettle of clean water to the boil. Add $1/4$ cup of Tide soap until it is dissolved. Place the material in and stir. When the water is deep with color, pour it out and start the process over again. Continue to do this until you have reached the shade you want or until all the color is removed. It is very important to rinse all the soap out of the material before you dry it or use to for dyeing. Do not be surprised if a different color appears when doing this. Many commercial dyers do not start out with white wool. That is why it is often so hard to match their colors.

■ **If your tap water is very "hard,"** it can have a big effect on the acid dyes used for wool. Acid dyes tend to float in hard water. If it is too soft, it can cause the dyes to fade or turn muddy. If you do not have a water softener for this condition, use a little "Calgon" or "Spic and Span" in your dye bath. Be careful to use just a bit—$1/2$ teaspoon for 2 gallons. PH strips are most useful in determining the condition of your water. On a scale of 1 to 12, the best range for dyeing is 5, 6 and 7.

■ **When you have to dye a big amount of background,** more than will fit in one pot, make sure to keep careful records on your first batch. On each successive batch, make sure to use exactly the same amount and kind of fabric, the same amount of clean kettle water as well as dye and mordant. Simmer it the same amount of time over the same heat. Also, if possible, do all the dyeing on the same day so that all of the tap water will be relatively the same. Even with this, you may have slight variations. This can be over come by tearing a section from each dyed piece as you do your cutting. Mix the cut pieces up as they are used. This way you are distributing all of the wool evenly through the rug.

■ **When color planning a rug,** choose colors that you like. Since we are all drawn to certain colors, it only stands to reason that it will be easier for us to work with colors we enjoy. So many rug hookers settle for colors that someone else picks for them. Consequently, they often loose interest and never finish their projects. A teacher is supposed to suggest and counsel a student. Ultimately, however, since you are the one that will have to live with it, you will be happier if you work to find suitable colors that you like.

JANE OLSON ON WOOL

■ **Cashmere wool** is wonderful to work with and soft. However, it will not wear as well over the years once worked into a floor rug.

■ **Rugs made of wider cuts** tend to wear better than those made with a #3. The narrower the strips are cut the more the material is weakened.

GENERAL HOOKING TIPS

■ **When hooking backgrounds,** be sure to use the same technique throughout the rug pattern. I hooked one of my patterns that had a plain center with straight hooking first. Bordering it was a wide band with the principle design. I hooked this in a curlicue technique. To my dismay the center would not lay flat even after several pressings. I finally reworked the center with a curlicue technique, and, viola, it laid flat. Mixing the two techniques was what caused the problem.

■ **Start in the center and work out.** This allows the backing to move out with you as you hook. If you start on the outside and work in, the backing has no place to go once encircled and will cause the rug to bubble when hooked.

■ **Starting in the center and working out** also helps if you run out of background wool. Since it is often very difficult to match a color exactly, we can find ourselves in a bind when we run out of wool half way through a project. When this

happens, you can replace your background wool at that point with a new shade of your color. Finger it in with the original wool and it will look like you planned it that way.

■ **After hooking a design,** hook one or two rows of background color around the design. This will hold the lines firm in the contour of the design.

■ **Repetition** sometimes becomes very boring, but this is what makes a beautiful flowing design.

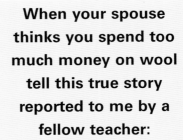

■ **You can mend the backing if a thread breaks.** Pull another thread from the outside edge of your pattern. Thread it through a large-eyed needle and weave it in the same channel as the broken thread. Weave it 4" longer on both ends to ensure that it will not come apart when hooking.

■ **Save your leftover cut pieces in a bag.** Some times, all you need is just two or three loops of another color to achieve a great effect. Keep your leftovers nearby and they will come in handy for your and your friends.

■ **Do not cut your selvage edges** for use in regular hooking. The color and texture of a selvage is different than the regular wool, causing the strips to be noticeable. Instead, tear them off before you cut and save them for a selvage project. Tearing them at the spot where the regular wool begins will give you a piece that is about ¹/₂" wide and perfect for

Jane Olson hooking at her frame.

primitive projects. They are particularly great for chair seats.

■ **When you are unhappy with a section** you have hooked, don't immediately rip it out. Keep working with the option of going back later. Often you will find that, with more hooking done, the offending section looks better than you thought it would. If it still bothers you, then take it out. Many hookers spend way too much time reverse hooking!

When your spouse thinks you spend too much money on wool tell this true story reported to me by a fellow teacher:

A rug hooker and braider had been buying so much wool that her husband complained it was taking up too much storage space in the house. As she bought even more wool, she began storing it in the trunk of the family car. One winter day, as they were on their way to Northern Wisconsin, an oncoming car veered into their lane and collided with them. The husband was thrown from the car and seriously injured. While awaiting the ambulance, the lady was able to use the wool in the trunk to cover her husband. Later, the doctor told him that his life had probably been saved because of his wife's quick thinking and all that wool! So, don't be afraid to buy a lot of wool. It may save your spouse's life.

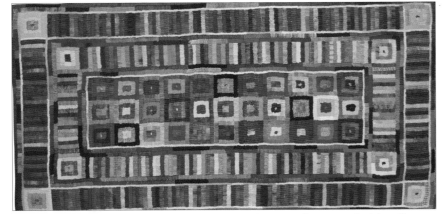

My Color Box, 59" x 44", #10-cut wool selvage strips on primitive linen. Designed and hooked by Gene Shepherd, 2004. This rug was made completely with selvage strips in a #10 cut. (The yellow line is a #8.) Because all the wool is very thick, it will wear evenly.

Categories of Hand-Hooked Rugs

Traditional Fine Shaded—Bowl of Flowers, 36" x 26", #3-cut of wool on rug warp using 6-value swatches. Adapted from "Blythe Schoals" by Margaret Masters. Hooked by Carla Fortney, 2004.

Rugs can be categorized in many ways. The simplest method is to just sort them by cut size. Cuts #2-4 are considered fine cuts. Medium cuts are those made with #5 and #6. Wide cuts begin with #7 and proceed to #10, which is $1/2$" wide. Some hand ripped pieces are even bigger. However, rug hookers usually want more descriptive categories than just cut size. While there is much discussion about what those categories should be, we list those styles, which we think are most appropriate.

Traditional Fine Shaded

This traditional style is characterized by, but not limited to, the use of swatches with six or more values and dip-dyes. These natural looking designs are most often composed of floral, fruit, and scroll motifs. Although traditionally made with cuts #3 and #4, designs with bigger motifs can be hooked with larger cuts.

Detailed Fine Cut

These realistic rugs, often used to portray animals, people, nature, and still life scenes, achieve their look through the use of many different colors and values instead of a predominant use of multi-valued swatches. They may be hooked flat or sculpted. The normal cut sizes for these rugs are #2-5.

Pictorial

Pictorial rugs capture a "snapshot" moment. They usually portray some story or event and can be hooked in any size cut. They run the gamut between realistic and cartoon representations. Pictorials can also employ lettering, sayings, or poems.

Oriental

A true Oriental Rug will tell a story through use of geometric designs, some floral motifs and Chinese characters—think Blue Willow china. While it can have some borders, they usually utilize lines which are more straight than fluid. These designs tend to not be as busy as their cousin, the Persian. Oriental rugs also have larger sections of plain open space in their design. These rugs can be done in cuts #2-8.

Persian

Persians tend to be a riot of flowers, scrolls, paisleys, and some geometric motifs, all presented in successive borders. Their lines are fluid and busy. The old Persians used only simple solid colors in red, blue, gold, and natural. These rugs can be done in cuts #2-8.

Crewel

English crewel embroidery provides the inspiration for this category of rug designs. The flowers and leaves are elegant and fanciful "padulas" (flowers invented for the design—it's recognized as a flower, even though it isn't a real flower) in vibrant and often unusual colors.

Primitive Wide Cut

With a nod to the earliest known examples of simple hooked rugs, these designs are constructed with the "wide brush strokes" of cuts #6-10. This style aims for representation, not realism.

Fancy Wide Cut

Realism does not have to be sacrificed when using a wide cut. When specialty-dye techniques or graphic use of three or four shade values are employed to their fullest effect, a fancy wide cut rug can produce a dramatic finished product. Even though they employ the widest "brush" strokes, these rugs still strive for realism, instead of simple representation. They are anything but primitive in their over all appearance.

Geometric Rugs

Geometric designs, one of the oldest categories of hooked rugs, are achieved by the repetition of and interaction between basic geometric elements. Adding all or parts of circles, triangles, rectangles, or other shapes in rigid sequence provides an unending series of design possibilities.

Mixed Media

When hooked pieces are made with non-traditional fibers, particularly the kind of materials that can not be walked on, the resulting work is considered mixed media. Since these works tend to be hung as art, almost anything can be used to achieve realism or effect.

Other

Some hooked rugs defy categories. It is also hard to compare other utilitarian objects like footstools or handbags with a room sized rug, thereby necessitating a general category for special items.

Traditional Fine Shaded—Savory Fruit, 33" x 42", #4- and #5 cut wool on monk's cloth. Designed by Jane Olson, Hooked by Norma Flodman, Worcester, Massachusetts, 1997. Dip dyes were used to hook everything in this rug except the background.

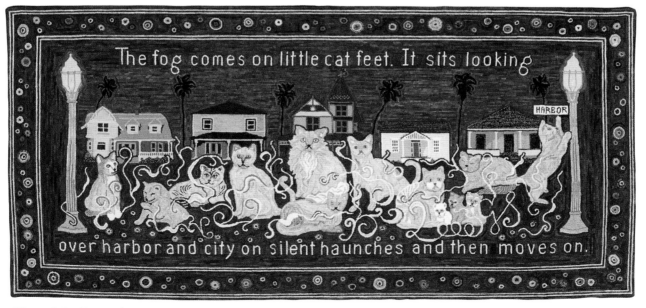

Pictorial—Fog 69½" x 33", #3- and 4-cut wool on rug warp. Designed and hooked by Gene Shepherd, Anaheim, California, 2001.

Detailed Fine-Cut—Pigtorial, 40" x 30", #3-cut wool on rug warp. Designed and hooked by Elizabeth Black, Bentonville, Virginia, 1999.

Detailed Fine Cut—The Ship, 30" x 24", #3-cut wool on monk's cloth. Designed and hooked by Jane Olson, Hawthorne, California, 1988.

Oriental—Ming Toy, 36" x 24", #3- and 5-cut wool on monk's cloth. Designed by Jane Olson. Hooked by Norma Flodman, Worcester, Massachusetts, 1992.

Persian—Kashan Roses, 39" x 27", #3- and # 4-cut wool on monk's cloth. Designed and hooked by Jane Olson, Hawthorne, California, 1995.

Persian Paisley, 60" x 84", #5-cut wool on monk's cloth. Designed and hooked by Jane Olson, 1983. Jane only used solid, off the bolt, red, blue, gold, and natural Dorr wool in a #5 cut to make this very traditional Persian rug.

Pictorial— The Covered Bridge, 36" x 24", #3-cut of wool on burlap. Designed and hooked by Jane Olson, Hawthorne, California, 1965.

Primitive Wide Cut—Fala Hates War, GRS, 26" round, #8- and #10-cut wool on monk's cloth. Recreated historic rug by Gene Shepherd, Anaheim, California, 2003. Except for the eyes, this simple Scottie is made from solid black wool and just a few strips of grey checked plaid.

Primitive Wide Cut—Bird's of a Feather, 36" x 24", #6 cut wool on monk's cloth. Designed by Jane Olson. Hooked by Jane Olson and Norma Flodman, Hawthorne, California, 2004.

Fancy Wide Cut—Mammoth Flowers, 96" x 36", #10-cut wool on linen. Designed by Harry M. Fraser, Co. Hooked by Anne Eastwood, Venice, Florida, 2002. The artist uses dip dyes to produce a stunning effect in this elegant rug.

Fancy Wide Cut—#1 Sheep, 40" x 32", hand cut wool on burlap. Designed by Land's End. Hooked by Gene Shepherd, Anaheim, California, 1998. Significant definition is achieved with just a few loops in three different values of plaid against the solid beige sheep.

Geometric—Untitled geometric, 54" x 37", #8-cut wool and mixed fabrics on burlap. Designer unknown. Hooked by Betty Weigle, Albion, Illinois, 1962. The artist broke with convention when hooking the curved shapes with straight lines in a somewhat random pattern. Black background makes this unusual approach work.

Geometric—Miss Weigle, 60" x 36", #6- and 8-cut wool on monk's cloth. Designed and hooked by Gene Shepherd, Anaheim, California, 2004. This design, based on circles, squares, and triangles, constantly finds new ways to repeat the motifs. A geometric design does not have to be a single "quilt block" design repeated over and over.

Mixed Media—Heather's Mermaid, 36" x 67", #4-8 cuts of wool, hand-cut wool, and mixed media on Hessian burlap. Designed and hooked by Heather Ritchie, Reeth, England, 2003. Wool fabric, satin, men's silk ties, Indian saris, costume jewelry, and wool roving are all used to great effect in this charming piece.

Mixed Media—Proddy Sheep, 19" x 22", #6- and hand-cut wool with roving, and metallic yarn on backing. Designed by Goat Hill Designs. Hooked by Bernice Herron, Huntington Beach, California, 2004. A three-dimensional effect is created with both the wool roving used for the sheep's head and the prodded flowers. Made of very large hand torn wool, the proddy pieces were rounded for additional interest. Flower centers were made with decorative yarns.

Other—Russian Birch, 29$\frac{1}{2}$" x 66", #2-10 cut wool on monk's cloth. Designed and hooked by Gene Shepherd, Anaheim, California, 2003. Since this rug utilizes all cuts from #2-10, it can not be classified exclusively as an example of fine, medium, or wide cuts. While it shares characteristics with both pictorials and geometrics, it is not a good example of either. "Other" seems the only appropriate designation.

Crewel—Jacobean Panel, 15" x 36", #3-cut of wool on monk's cloth. Designed by Mildred Sprout. Hooked by Susan Andreson, Newport Beach, California, 2005.

CHAPTER 9

Rugger's Roundtable

SPECIAL EDITION

Rugger's Roundtable by *Jane Olson*

30–YEAR ANNIVERSARY EDITION
DECEMBER 2005

Jane Olson Rug Studio
Tel 310-643-5902 • Fax 310-643-7367

www.janeolsonrugstudio.com
P.O. Box 351 • Hawthorne, CA 90250

#300 **TWIN ROSES**
26″ x 46″

shp wt 1-1/2 lb

TWIN ROSES is a design by *Jane Olson* and *Gene Shepherd* made especially for the book *"The Rug Hooker's Bible"*.

This rug pattern can be worked as a primitive or a traditional.

The borders surrounding the roses give one a chance to work key-designs, squares, circles and triangles.

The color balance of the pattern is achieved by using the same colors in the borders as in the roses and leaves.

It is a pattern that can be enjoyed by a beginner or an experienced rug hooker.

TWIN ROSES is about 8 sq ft. The material required is 4 lbs or 5 to 6 yards.

For a primitive rug, I suggest using a #6 or #8 cut. A variation would be a #6 cut on the design and a #8 cut on the background and border.

For a traditional rug, I suggest using a #4 cut for the design and a #5 cut for the background and border.

•

Monk's Cloth-$79.95
Primitive Linen-$99.95

All back issues of the Rugger's Roundtable are available as *Individual* copies or:

Page 01

PRIMITIVE ROSE

The rose is hooked with the 3 shades of **NUGGET GOLD** and **CHERRY**.

The diagram shows where to work the 3 shades. These are the same 3 shades that are used in the designs surrounding the roses.

The leaves are worked with 3 shades. The first 2 shades are **GREEN** and the third shade is a very **DARK CHERRY**.

The veins in the **GREEN** leaves are worked with **DARK CHERRY** and vice versa.

Outline all petals and leaves with dyed tweed.

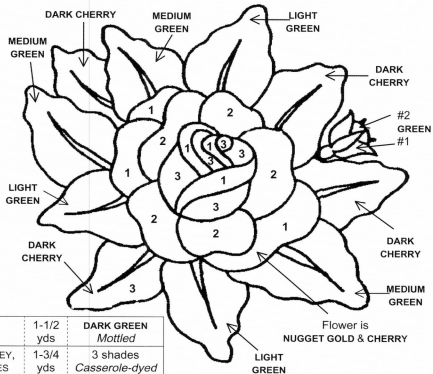

BACKGROUND & BORDER	1-1/2 yds	**DARK GREEN** *Mottled*
ROSES, BLOCKS, GREEK KEY, INSIDE TRIANGLE & CIRCLES	1-3/4 yds	3 shades *Casserole-dyed*
LEAVES, GREEK KEY, OUTSIDE TRIANGLES & CIRCLES	1-3/4 yds	3 shades *Casserole-dyed*
OUTLINE	1 yd	Dyed tweed w/ Flower dyes

——— **Cut 3-1/2 yards into 1/4-yard pieces** ———
**Use (7) 1/4-yd pieces for Flowers & Border designs.
Use (7) 1/4-yd pieces for Leaves & Border designs**.

1/4 tsp **NUGGET GOLD**	1/2 cup hot water
1-1/2 tsp **CHERRY**	1-1/2 cup hot water

CASSEROLE DYEING FOR FLOWERS & BORDERS

Tear the 1-1/2 yards into 1/2-yard pieces and again to result in 1/4-yard pieces. Wet these pieces in hot water and a little liquid detergent.

First Shade—*two pieces*

Use a large casserole pan. Place one piece in the pan containing 2 to 3 inches of simmering water and 1/4 cup of white vinegar. Spot several tbsp of **NUGGET GOLD** over the material. Let these colors flow into each other.

After a minute or so, spot with 1 or 2 tbsp of **CHERRY**. Repeat this on the next piece. Add a little more water and cover with foil. Simmer for 20 minutes or place in the oven at 300° for 30 minutes.

Second Shade—*two pieces*

Place one piece in the pan containing 2 to 3 inches of simmering water and 1/4 cup of white vinegar. Spot with 3 or 4 tbsp of **NUGGET GOLD** and let it flow together. Spot this with 5 or 6 tbsp of **CHERRY**. Repeat this for the next piece. Use the same setting procedure as for the first shade.

Third Shade—*three pieces*

After placing the first piece in the casserole, use 1 or 2 tbsp of **NUGGET GOLD** and then use 8 or 9 tbsp of **CHERRY**. Repeat this for the next 2 pieces. Proceed with the setting procedure.

INSTRUCTIONS FOR CASSEROLE DYING OF LEAVES & BORDER DESIGNS ARE ON THE NEXT PAGE.

1/8 tsp **RESEDA GREEN**	1/8 tsp **BRIGHT GREEN** & 1/8 tsp **BRONZE**	1/2 cup hot water
1/4 tsp **RESEDA GREEN**	1/4 tsp **BRIGHT GREEN** & 1/4 tsp **BRONZE**	1 cup hot water
1 tsp **CHERRY**	1/2 cup hot water	

CASSEROLE DYING FOR LEAVES & BORDER DESIGNS

Use the same amount of material, tearing as for the flowers.

First Shade—*two pieces*

Use a large casserole pan. Place one piece in the pan containing 2 to 3 inches of simmering water and 1/4 cup of white vinegar. Spoon 4 tbsp from the first cup of dye. Repeat this for the next piece, using all the 1/2 cup of dye. Cover with foil and proceed with the setting procedure as on the previous page.

Second Shade—*two pieces*

Place the first piece in the simmering vinegar water and use 1/2 cup of the second mixture of **GREEN** dye. Repeat this for the next piece and proceed as above.

Third Shade—*three pieces*

Place the first piece in the casserole of simmering vinegar water and use 1/2 cup of **CHERRY**, spotting it here and there. Repeat this for the next 2 pieces and proceed with the setting procedure.

PRIMITIVE BORDERS

Outline all lines with 1 yard dyed tweed or check material

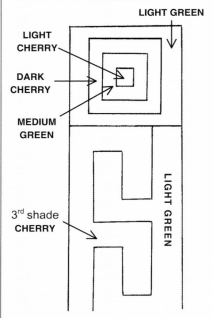

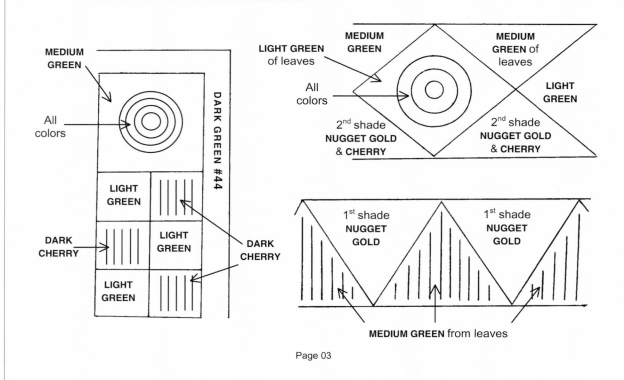

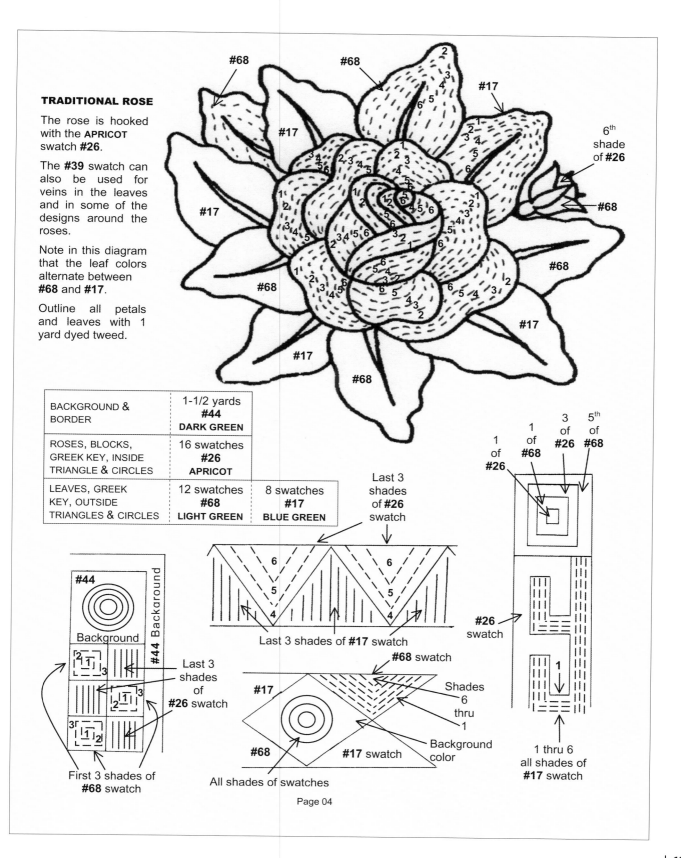

TRADITIONAL ROSE

The rose is hooked with the **APRICOT** swatch **#26**.

The **#39** swatch can also be used for veins in the leaves and in some of the designs around the roses.

Note in this diagram that the leaf colors alternate between **#68** and **#17**.

Outline all petals and leaves with 1 yard dyed tweed.

BACKGROUND & BORDER	1-1/2 yards **#44** DARK GREEN	
ROSES, BLOCKS, GREEK KEY, INSIDE TRIANGLE & CIRCLES	16 swatches **#26** APRICOT	
LEAVES, GREEK KEY, OUTSIDE TRIANGLES & CIRCLES	12 swatches **#68** LIGHT GREEN	8 swatches **#17** BLUE GREEN

Last 3 shades of **#26** swatch

Last 3 shades of **#17** swatch

#68 swatch

Shades 6 thru 1

Background color

#26 swatch

1 thru 6 all shades of **#17** swatch

1 of **#26**

1 of **#68**

3 of **#26**

5th of **#68**

#44

Background

#44 Backaround

Last 3 shades of **#26** swatch

First 3 shades of **#68** swatch

#17

#68

#17 swatch

All shades of swatches

FROM JANE OLSON

It's no secret I love Rug Hooking. I love to get up early in the morning and start dyeing wool. I love to design new patterns and then can't wait to begin hooking them. I love the way new rug designs can pop up in my mind while enjoying nature, listening to a client's need or sitting, once again, in e-fensive riving School (seems my right foot is a bit on the heavy side)! I love to teach be-ginning rug hookers and I love to teach those who have been hooking as long as I have. I love to walk on rugs in my own home and I love to walk on them in the homes of my children and grandchildren. I love everything about rug hooking and never seem to get tired of it or other people who also love rug hooking.

I am not sure if I found Rug Hooking or if it found me. All I know is that in early 1950's, while coping with the demands of running a busy home for a talented husband and three small children, I needed some sort of per-sonal creative outlet. Almost by accident, I stumbled into a hooking group that reac-quainted me with this art form, but unlike my childhood memories of the boring hours spent hooking my mother's backgrounds, it provided the creative outlet I craved. It's not only that rug hooking gave me something creative to do, but it also lifted my spirits.

Norma Flodman   Gene Shepherd   Jane Olson

I needed to "create" and couldn't wait for every spare minute after the housework was done or the kids were in bed that allowed me this exhilarating experience. I still feel that way and hope that Rug Hooking will also lift and soothe your spirit.

Nothing pleases me more than to see the increasing popularity that rug hooking is enjoying. I particu-larly like to see those artists who break new ground and find unique ways of doing things with wool and hook. Isn't it great to be a part of such a dynamic art form? I'm equally happy to see so many new teachers cropping up all over the nation. It's particularly satisfying to see my former stu-dents "hang up their shingle". When I see this sort of enthusiasm I know our art form is in good hands for years to come.

Finally, I couldn't be happier with how things have come together for this book project. Gene Shepherd not only edited and organ-ized my *Rugger's Roundtable* in a way that pleased me, he contributed substantial original material as well. It has been a thrill to see the whole thing come together under his direction. The entire project has been a pleasure. I hope you enjoy it. *Jane*

RUG TIP

Since so much of this book already includes many hooking tips from me, it seemed appropriate to ask my sister Norma to share some of her expertise on the subject. For many years she has traveled with me to workshops and camps and is always in demand for her special talent for humor and wit:

"If you want to dramatically improve your hooking at a workshop or camp, make sure you sit next to the worst rug hooker in the room. Their poor hooking will make your work look better. Never sit next to a good hooker because it will make your work look bad."

Norma Flodman

RESOURCES

■ **Jane Olson**
www.janeolsonrugstudio.com

■ **Gene Shepherd**
www.geneshepherd.com or
gene@geneshepherd.com

■ *Rug Hooking* **Magazine**
www.rughookingonline.come
rughook@paonline.com

Our Favorite Tools:

The Bliss Model A

■ **Fraser Rug Making Equipment**
(336) 573-9830
www.fraserrugs.com

The Townsend Cutter

Stainless Steel Rug Hooking Frame)

■ **Townsend Industries, Inc.**
(877) 868-3544
www.townsendfabric
cutter.com

■ **Kay's Creations**
800.727.3769
www.kscreations.com

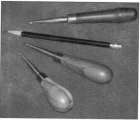

Hartman Hook

■ **Hartman's Hooks**
(330) 653-9730
www.HartmansHook.
com

■ **Waldoboro Designs and Instruction**
Jacqueline Hansen
(207) 883-5403
www.rughookers
network.com/han
sen/1840

■ **The Dorr Mill Store**
(800) 846-3677
www.dorrmillstore.
com
dorrmillstore@nhvt.
net

ACKNOWLEDGEMENTS

We gratefully acknowledge the significant contributions of our friends, family, students and colleagues in the production of this book. Each went above and beyond the call of duty!

Florence Aguinaldo
Susan Andreson
Elizabeth Black
Kristi Boren
Anna Boyer
Marny Cardin
Jean Coon
Jacqueline Hansen
Bernice Herron

Anne Eastwood
Norma Flodman
Carla Fortney
JoAnn Gonzalez
Susan Madrigal
Susan Naples
Peggy Johnson
Susan Kievman
Marilyn Orbeck

Robin Page
Norma Piper
Lisa Rueger
Heather Ritchie
Marguerite Ryan
Sharon Saknit
Iris Salter
Ann Shepherd
Bessie Shepherd

Marsha Shepherd
Arlene Taromina
Betty Weigle
Annie Wilson
Jan Winter
Marion Wise

Likewise, the enthusiasm and confidence of J. Richard Noel, (Publisher, Stackpole, Inc.) and Virginia P. Stimmel, (Editor, *Rug Hooking* magazine) continues to undergird the growth and development of rug hooking on an international level. Their efforts, along with those of their staff, are both appreciated and applauded.

TWIN ROSES

Design by Jane Olson and Gene Shepherd.
Instructions for hooking this design are on pages 178–181.

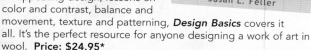